HOUSE PLANTS

LOVE, CARE AND REPAIR

ALYS FOWLER

This book is dedicated to Clare Savage

An Hachette UK Company
www.hachette.co.uk

First published as *Plant Love* in Great Britain in 2017.
This edition published in 2023 by Kyle Books,
an imprint of Octopus Publishing Group Ltd
Carmelite House
50 Victoria Embankment
London, EC4Y 0DZ
www.kylebooks.co.uk

10 9 8 7 6 5 4 3 2 1

ISBN 9781804191040

Distributed in the US by Hachette Book Group, 1290 Avenue of the Americas, 4th and 5th Floors, New York, NY 10104

Distributed in Canada by Canadian Manda Group, 664 Annette St., Toronto, Ontario, Canada M6S 2C8

Designer: Damian Jaques
Photographer: Simon Wheeler
Illustrations: Christian Tate
Project Editor: Sophie Allen
Copy Editor: Charlie Ryrie
Editorial Assistant: Isabel Gonzalez-Prendergast
Production: Nic Jones, Gemma John and Lisa Pinnell

* All photography by Simon Wheeler, except p75: Friedrich Strauss/GAP Photos; p76: Arsami/Shutterstock.com; p148: Avalon/Photoshot License/Alamy Stock Photo; p151: Damian Jacques; p157: Piya Sarutnuwat/Alamy Stock Photo

A Cataloguing in Publication record for this title is available from the British Library.

Printed and bound in China.

CONTENTS

PLANT INDEX

NATURAL ENVIRONMENT

Rocky

Forest/Rainforest

Desert

Boggy

SUN

POSITION

INTRODUCTION

Let it be said, clearly and simply, your plants do not want to live with you. They want to live in a tropical rainforest or cool desert or mountain ravine. They want to feel the breeze, taste soft rain, sleep when the sun goes down, a fair few of them would like to be in touch with their friends rather than living in a pot on their own. They'd like to be home, just not in your home.

They can't communicate this to you, yet, but they can and do communicate. They send out over 500 different chemical signals in a day; we just can't quite understand them all at the moment. If and when we do get to that point I like to think they'll be an amenable bunch. They may not want to be housebound, but they can certainly adapt to being so. But just in case they turn out to be very angry with us – and in general they have every right to be – perhaps it would be wisest to practise being as kind as possible to our house guests. Which means we should truly try to understand their needs.

I say this because too often plants' needs are talked about in such basic terms: water, light, and food. In this, all the subtle shifts and nuances of their lives and the ecology of their native habitats are lost. Understanding where they come from and how they have evolved leads to a far more empathetic understanding of their wants. Too often I see houseplants suffering because we'd like them to be something else – a decoration, an immobile furnishing, something to soften our inanimate interiors – rather than seeing them as something living that can flourish or flounder.

On the other hand, I know there are many humans who think of their houseplants as good friends and fellow dwellers and love them with a crazy affection that perhaps no garden plant would receive. I am one of them. I have houseplants that have travelled to every house I have lived in as an adult, seen me through breakups, soldiered on when I neglected them and rewarded me by flowering and new growth when I've repented my ways. These plants may grow wonky and a

little too leggy from too little light, they may never see the conditions they really need, they may never flower, may never have a pollinator visit them, may never get to set seed. Yet their selfless ways bring me such joy. They make a house a home, they change and grow, they wave at us when we come home[1], bring a room to life by saying someone lives here, invests in this space, cares for it, tends and grows in it.

Not only do they instil a sense of belonging to a space, but they are good for our indoor environment. There is considerable research from the likes of NASA and others to show that houseplants clean our air from pollutants, such as volatile organic compounds (VOCs). These VOCs are released from the many other things we furnish our homes with: computers, televisions, carpets, glues that hold our furniture together, from burning wood and cooking, from the flame retardants and pesticides used on our soft furnishing. They are found in the chemicals we use to clean our homes and in the cosmetics we use on our bodies. They are not good for our health and to live in an environment that has less of them makes sense. Healthy plants remove these compounds from the air, filtering them out through their roots as well as their leaves and releasing oxygen back into our environment. Plants are very effective air filters; this is how our atmosphere on this planet works. We wouldn't be able to breathe without the green life in our world.

Plants are not only important in our homes as air filters, they affect our health and wellbeing in many subtle ways. We respond to green and growth, to the biological details, the patterns and designs; we are fascinated by the intricacy of life, even if we don't recognise this. We evolved with plants, in a rich

---

[1] Maranthaceae family do actually wave; they move their leaves diurnally to catch the best light and thus can often be seen waving goodnight.

biodiverse environment and just looking at plants, let alone interacting with them, has a positive benefit on our wellbeing, on how our system functions. If you have ever stopped to smell a flower or got lost in the detail of light playing on a leaf or a particularly pretty pattern, it's not just an aesthetic delight that's enticing you closer, it's a sort of internal mindfulness at play. The chemicals plants release, their scents and compounds interact with us on a cellular level. Clearly poisonous elements are no good for us, a warning to leave the plant alone, but there are many more, such as limonols and terpenes, that have an amazing effect on our systems, lowering and fighting free radicals and promoting our immune systems.

And here we have it. They may not want us, but we want them, indeed we need them. Lining every windowsill, hanging off shelves, towering next to book cases, cascading from ceilings, cleaning our air from pollutants, scenting it with the smell of green growth and pleasing our visual senses. I believe that indoor gardening is just as important and relevant as gardening outside. I see indoor plant lovers as gardeners every bit as enthusiastic and loving as outdoor ones.

SO HOW DO WE TRY TO KEEP OUR LONG-TERM HOUSEGUESTS HAPPY? UNDERSTAND THE RULES

Plants do have a few basic needs: they must receive light to photosynthesise and produce energy, they must have water, they must have nutrients and many must have soil to anchor their roots in. Within these boundaries are vast planes of difference. A desert cactus comes from a completely different world to an understorey tropical plant, yet you can get both to grow in your house, possibly even next door to each other.

A plant grown in a pot is almost entirely reliant on you for all its water and food needs and an indoor plant also relies on you for how much and what kind of light it receives. You can play god with houseplants, endlessly taking them to the brink and reviving them at the last

minute, but it doesn't exactly make for a healthy plant.

Plants need many things to thrive, but they need two things to stay alive: water and light. Both of these are required for photosynthesis, where plants utilise carbon dioxide, water and light to create carbohydrates and oxygen. The more light there is the more water is required to photosynthesise. However, there is a limitation as many hot places are not wet or wet enough to keep the photosynthesis equation running at full pelt. In hot and dry conditions, plants close their stomata (the breathing pores in all leaves) to prevent water loss. When this happens, carbon dioxide will decrease, limiting the equation further and resulting in an increase of oxygen, which in turn causes an increase in respiration. That's why many outdoor plants wilt on a hot day; they are just not adapted to keep up with the ever-spiralling equation.

Some plants, including most of your houseplants, have evolved mechanisms to increase the carbon dioxide concentration in their leaves under these conditions.

Plants differ in the way they carry out photosynthesis to convert light to energy and carbon dioxide in the air to carbohydrates, by fixing carbon in different ways. Tropical plants have a mechanism called C4 carbon fixation, which means that as long as there's water, rising temperatures don't mean growth will slow down. They produce considerably more sugar than cool season or temperate plants, which use a C3 mechanism allowing them to grow at rapid rates in hot conditions.

If there's not enough water, but even hotter conditions, then another group of plants, namely cacti and succulents, use something called CAM, Crassulacean Acid Metabolism. Here these plants do something entirely opposite to every other plant on the earth. Those stomata, the breathing pores, are only opened at night in CAM plants. They allow carbon dioxide to enter and be fixed as organic acids. Then during the day, when the stomata are closed to prevent water loss, they take those acids and turn them back into carbon dioxide so they can photosynthesise. This means they

can survive in very high temperatures with low and/ or infrequent water conditions (those fleshy leaves are storing water for this reason).

Some plants are hybrids between the three methods of photosynthesis, switching between C3 and CAM or C4 and CAM under periods of drought or stress.

Some of your houseplants will be either C4 or CAM and these adaptations mean that they can live in our warm houses or be left on a bright, hot windowsill and survive despite your erratic watering.

The main thing you need to take from this is that in sunny, hot conditions plants will need more water, particularly if they are big, leafy tropical plants that use C4 mechanisms. On cloudy days or during the winter when the light levels are low, whatever mechanism the plant uses, it will need less water. A plant growing on a windowsill without bright light will need less watering than one growing in bright conditions.

If you find yourself unable to keep up with watering a plant, then moving it away from the light source will slow down its growth and reduce the amount of water it needs. This is a good method if you're going away for a bit – move your plants to slightly shadier conditions and they will require less water and grow more slowly.

One commonly held mistaken belief about houseplants is putting them in a pot with no drainage. You can do this and I am sure any houseplant aficionado has an example of a plant growing in such pot. However, this severely limits how well the plant will grow, shortens its life span and requires you to be very attentive with watering. All roots require oxygen to survive. They need this just as much as the parts of the plants above ground. Roots need to breathe and soils that are depleted of oxygen due to compaction or flooding support less healthy plants unless they are specifically adapted to live in such conditions, such as bog and water plants. Without air the compost in your drainage-free pots will very quickly turn anaerobic. The roots, particularly at the bottom where the water accumulates, will start to rot off and the plant will concentrate on growing roots in the top layer of the pot.

Soil that has become anaerobic has fewer available nutrients and roots that are forced to grow near the surface of the compost become congested and run the risk of drying out quicker, particularly if they are, say, sitting above a radiator.

You might hear that you can get away with misting the plant. Misting is never the same as watering. Often the kind of plants grown in drainage-free pots are succulents and cacti that really don't want to be misted.

In short, use a pot with drainage; it's better for the plant and easier for you to maintain. If you have a decorative pot that you are keen to use, you can either use a a plastic pot inside the decorative one over a layer of pebbles or Leca – clay balls designed for such purposes – or you can drill drainage holes into your pot using a drill suitable for ceramic tiles.

Even plants grown in pots with drainage will need a little care to make sure the soil stays properly aerated. Compost in pots naturally compacts over time. This is partly due to watering and partly because compost is

not soil and is still in a process of decomposing. As compost is largely composed of organic matter, it is still rotting down and as this happens it sinks and compacts. In nature, worms and other soil organisms aerate soil as they make their burrows and homes and so compacting doesn't happen. However, you are unlikely to have or want worms in your house, so you have to act like one instead.

Repotting your plant is a good way to make sure the compost stays fluffy, but as you may only need to do this every two years or so, in the meantime you can take a chopstick or similar implement and poke holes carefully around the top of your pot, going down as far as you can without damaging the roots, wiggling the chopstick around, so that you aerate the pot. These air channels will provide the roots with fresh oxygen and ensure that water drains through the pot faster. You can do this to any pot plant, and it makes sense to do this regularly to plants that particularly favour free-draining conditions. Succulents, cacti and lithophytes (plants that grow on rocks) prefer soils that drain incredibly

quickly and their fine root hairs rot off in moist soils.

Lastly, you can unwittingly have a huge effect on the growth of the roots by poor watering habits. A healthy plant has just as much going on below as it does above. A healthy root mass allows the plant to survive all sorts of ups and downs – drought, temperature extremes, pest attack – so you want your plants to have the healthiest roots possible. Healthy roots tend to be white, a little translucent and plump. The soil should smell fresh and the roots should reach throughout the pot, but should not be spiralling or shooting out of the drainage holes at the bottom. Unhealthy roots often look rotten, are an unhealthy yellow or black, don't snap, but sort of smear away when you tug at them and the soil often smells anaerobic or a little rotting, partly because the roots are rotting in it.

Plants grow roots to anchor themselves and to find food and water. Thus, a healthy plant has adventurous roots that wish to explore all their territory. One way to make sure they do this is to water well; if you just give the plant a tiny bit of water, a sprinkling and no more,

then the roots learn to grow where they can absorb the water quickly. This often means the roots grow in the top couple of centimetres of the soil and nowhere else. As stated, this isn't great because the roots only have a limited space to absorb nutrients and water and because roots that grow on the surface are liable to dry out quicker and get burnt in hot conditions and frozen in very cold ones. Therefore, whatever the plants watering needs are, it is important to water enough that it drains out through the bottom. It may then be necessary to throw away this water in the saucer (or use it for the next door houseplant) so that the plant doesn't sit in water. Actively making sure that the soil has good drainage through the addition of perlite, grit, or making holes in the compost will ensure that the water runs through the soil in a suitable manner. If you know that the plant likes to remain in moist soil, then less grit or perlite is used and sometimes more absorbent material like bark mulch is added.

Mulching the top of the pot with decorative pebbles or grit is also a good idea because this will help lock in water and stop it being lost to evaporation and, to some extent, this helps to stop compost gnats, those annoying little flies that you often get with houseplants. They are looking to lay their eggs in damp organic matter, and grit is far from that.

IF YOUR PLANT DRIES OUT

Cheap houseplants are often grown largely in peat, which is not good for the environment. Peat is a precious resource that is depleted worldwide. It also is not necessarily good for the plant, it tends to have little or no nutrient value, and, worse still, it dries to the bone if neglected. You'll know if your plant is largely in peat because if it is allowed to get very dry it will lift entirely out of the pot and be difficult to rewet. One solution is to immerse the entire pot in a bucket of water and, if the compost doesn't look like it is rewetting quickly enough, add just a drop or two of washing-up liquid,. This will break the surface tension between the water and the soil and allow the soil to absorb water quickly. You will see bubbles start to appear as air is pushed out between the soil particles. When the bubbles stop take the plant out and allow it to drain. Fresh oxygen-rich air will then be drawn back into the pot and, if it's not on the brink, the plant will revive.

LIGHT AND HOW IT ENTERS A ROOM

Light is life for a plant. If there's too little there is not enough energy for them to grow. What is the right amount of light for your plant? Even with artificial light it is very hard to reproduce the right amount of the plant's native habitat, particularly of desert conditions. There is never going to be as much light indoors as there is outdoors, even in a glasshouse. In a house, your rooms will vary according to which way they face and the size of the window, and also by factors such as the colour of the wall. The general rule of thumb is that there is strong direct light at the window, depending on the direction it faces, and then good indirect light up to 1.5–1.8m (6–8ft) away from it. The rest of the room is in shade, though the walls will bounce light around and bright, light walls are obviously better at doing this than dark ones. Mirrors will bounce light around and artificial lights will add a little more, though the wattage of most house lights is too low to provide much help.

South-facing windows are the brightest, then east, then west-facing. The light will vary during the day and might be blocked out at certain points of the year. The light from a north-facing window is the least bright, but the steadiest. Big skylights offer some of the best conditions because the plant will receive a shower of light. To some extent your plant will tell where the strongest light is coming from because light from only one direction will cause it to bend to that direction, which is why it's important to turn your plants around if you can, so that they remain straight(ish) and upright.

Rooms that are south-facing are bright and hot. In summer, some cacti and succulents are the few plants that can take such bright conditions, particularly on the windowsill. At around 90cm (3ft) away from a south-facing window many of your tropical, purple-leaved and variegated plants will thrive. But some, such as *Maranta* and begonias, will still find this light too bright as these are understorey plants and direct light rarely travels to them in their natural habitat. On the whole, variegated plants need more light than green ones because they have less chlorophyll, the green cells for photosynthesis, and the green parts have to work harder. Variegated plants that are turning or reverting to green are telling you that they are not getting enough light.

East-facing windows get morning sun, which will not scorch plants for most of the year, except in summer. One metre (3ft) or so away from an east-facing window is ideal for many shade-loving tropical plants. West-facing windows can get as hot as south-facing windows – they are suitable for a wide range of houseplants that like bright light, particularly as they stay lighter for longer than other windows and thus warmer too. This is an ideal location for plants like philodendrons, Swiss cheese plants (*Monstera deliciosa*) and rubber plants

(*Ficus elastica*). They are also great for many cacti and succulents that will tolerate the direct summer light. North-facing windows tend to have a gentle, unvarying light, which is perfect for shade-loving plants.

But whichever window you choose, it's important to stress that, as the light comes from only one direction, the plants will need to be turned. Even shade-loving plants in the wild get light, if indirect, from many directions, particularly from above. In the winter, it makes sense to move any plants that are away from the window closer to compensate for the lower seasonal light levels.

Ceiling lights can provide valuable extra light for tropical plants that are used to days and nights of equal length. However, spotlights and side lights can get too hot for most plants, particularly if they are close to them. You can supplement with daylight bulbs if you want to be specially kind to your plants. There are horticultural lights that tend to have a particular sort of glow that throws a wider spectrum to plants, but they look a little odd in houses.

UNDERSTAND WHERE YOUR PLANTS COME FROM

Most people's houses are around 16–25°C/60–77°F, with the majority around 21°C/70°F in the winter, when heating is required. There are fluctuations: at night, when people are at work and changes in the outside weather, but on the whole houses are warm environments and the plants that live in them have to like this. Therefore, it's no surprise that our houseplants broadly fall into two categories. They are either from the tropics or from desert, semi-desert or other hot, dry places. The tropical lot tend to like humid conditions and the dry lot obviously don't like damp conditions, but are happy instead with our brightest windowsills and dry central heating.

No one particularly wants a hot, humid house as damp rots many of our building materials. Tropical plants can do well in our houses despite not having quite the humidity they require because they all tend to be understorey plants of the rainforest, which means they are very good at surviving in our dark interiors. The understorey plants in the rainforest receive little, if no, direct light; 95 per cent is absorbed by the canopy and the quality of the wavelengths that do get through are greatly impoverished, particularly those required for efficient photosynthesis. For this reason, the highly shiny, deep green leaves and purple undersides of many of these plants are all adaptations to bouncing light around on the top side and absorbing light from the far end of the spectrum below. Understorey plants are masters at utilising wavelengths that canopy plants can't.

The forest understorey also experiences higher humidity than exposed areas. As light can't get through to the bottom of the forest floor, the ground does not heat up or cool down as rapidly as open ground. This means that the ground dries out very slowly, in fact it remains pretty much moist all the time. Tropical ferns, mosses and epiphytes (plants that grow harmlessly on other plants) thrive in these areas because of the greater humidity. Epiphytes in the rainforest live mostly on tree trunks and branches to make the most of the sunlight in the canopy layer.

The sort of plants that love such humid conditions will love your warm bathroom, but have a harder time sitting in your warm but dry sitting room. One way to get around this is to sit the plant in a tray of pebbles and water to improve humidity. Grouping your plants together will also help to create a microclimate – plants are very good at keeping the spaces between themselves nicely humid as they respire.

Tropical rainforest plants have leaf adaptations to withstand their humid homes. Algae grow very quickly in such conditions and as leaves are essentially solar panels it does the plant no favours if they get covered in gunk; it means they can't work as effectively. Many tropical plants have drip tips – pointed tips to the end of the leaf – and waxy surfaces that ensure that excess water runs off easily. This is important because a build-up of water would create ideal conditions for algae to grow on the leaves, which would block out sunlight and reduce the plants' ability to photosynthesise.

Some leaves have a completely different approach. The leaves of the staghorn fern or air plants, for instance, have a furry covering of hairs, known as trichomes, specially adapted to catch water, allowing the plants slowly to absorb it and any nutrient run-off. Plants with these kinds of leaves tend to have roots that are merely anchors while their leaves do the feeding and absorbing of water.

The leaves are also often arranged at different angles, moving if necessary on a daily basis, so that the plant

avoids shading its own leaves. In some plants, such as *Monstera deliciosa*, the Swiss cheese plant, the leaves change shape depending on what height they are growing on the plant. The lower leaves are full, but the leaves higher up have holes in them to let light and water through.

The bright, intense light and sporadic rainfall in the desert require a completely different set of adaptations. Here the plant must concentrate on trying to store water until the next rain comes. Succulents and cacti often have grey-green or pale silver leaves that help to reflect light, and this colour means that the plant doesn't get quite so hot. Some desert plants have hairy leaves that again protect the plant from extremes of heat and cold – desert temperatures can drop dramatically at night. The hairs also act like a kind of sunscreen. The growing tip tends to be the hairiest as this is the most vulnerable spot on the plant.

Cacti and succulent leaves are often thick with a waxy cuticle and protective layer on the surface, again to prevent water loss. The leaves and stems are also adapted to store water. Barrel cactus, for example, will swell to store as much water as possible. They typically have rounded or re-curved leaves that minimise the surface area that receives light.

In cacti, the leaves have been done away with and replaced with spines (that are technically modified leaves). The spines do two things: they protect the fleshy parts that are so desirable to thirsty herbivores, and they shade the stem. Fishhook cacti have re-curved spines that are arranged densely around the growing tip for this reason. Some desert plants, like *Euphorbia*, have toxic sap to deter insects and herbivores from eating them.

The roots of desert plants are also adapted to make the most of any water. They tend to fall into two camps: shallow root systems that collect the small amount of water, mainly dew, that occurs overnight or they have extremely deep root systems that allow the plant to tap into underground water.

In very hot deserts where the daytime temperature is too high for many insects to fly, flowering tends to only happen at night to attract moths and others that fly in the cooler night temperatures, or very early in the morning, when the sun hasn't reached its highest point. The flowers tend to be pale, so they glow in moonlight.

Probably my favourite leaf adaptations are known as fenestrations, derived from the Latin for window. It is exactly that, a little epidermal window made up of a translucent area where sunlight can enter into the interior of the leaf so photosynthesis can occur. This primary function is to allow the plant to bury itself in the soil thereby minimising the exposure of the leaf surface area to the outside world, while the window allows unobstructed light to enter, be captured and utilised for photosynthesis without the whole leaf having to be exposed to the sun. You see this in *Lithops*, stone plants, and *Frithia*.

However, windows also appear in other plants that grow above ground, such as *Haworthia, Senecio* and desert-dwelling *Peperomia*. The leaves of these plants may be rolled or rounded to minimise water loss and it is thought that the windows are to compensate for the reduction in light interception. The window lets light into the interior to allow for as much photosynthesis as possible. The windows look particularly beautiful if you hold them up to light, like miniature stained-glass panels allowing you to peer into the inner world of the plant.

SEE THEM IN THEIR FULL GLORY

It's quite amazing to see your houseplants in their true wild habitats, but not everyone can get to a Brazilian rainforest or a Mexican desert. However, many cities have botanic gardens and conservatories where you can see your houseplants, if not exactly set free, at least growing to their full height. It's a lovely way to spend a day and you may learn a thing or two about growing conditions. In Kew Gardens you can see Swiss cheese plant, *Monstera deliciosa,* reaching to the top of the ceiling of its glasshouse, find cacti that you previously thought of as miniature plants as ripe, statuesque old-aged pensioners, and masses of others are trailing, creeping and clinging over tropical trees, providing a valuable understanding of what a tropical rainforest ecology looks like.

GIVE THEM ROOM TO GROW

Once you've seen them growing in more unfettered conditions, you might realise that you are unwittingly bonsaiing many of your houseplants. It's very easy to keep them thwarted by never repotting them. Most houseplants have made it onto the popular list because they are tough sorts that can hang out in difficult conditions and still get on with life. However, keeping a plant potbound does make work harder for you; it will dry out quicker, often fails to flower and can be more susceptible to pests. The health of the roots is paramount to the health of the overall plant.

REPOTTING

It's easy to tell when a plant needs repotting. If you lift it up and see roots come out of the drainage hole, this is a sure indication that the plant has used up all the available space in the pot and is searching for more nutrients and water. Cacti and slow-growing succulents such as Aeoniums and Sedums will take a number of years to reach this stage, particularly if they are in a decent-sized pot (rather than those ridiculous tiny pots that you buy at the petrol station). Tropical plants tend to be faster growing and if the plant is the sort that can reach several metres plus in the wild, then repotting often will reward you with bigger plants.

If you don't want your plant to grow too big it's better to prune the plant, including the roots, rather than keeping in constricted in a small pot. Some plants resent being moved and I've earmarked these in their descriptions.

On the whole, it is best to repot in late winter or early spring, when the plant is coming back into growth, as this means it won't sit in a large slump of wet soil. It's also wise not to jump too many pot sizes up at once. It takes time for roots to explore new soil and while this is happening, empty compost will remain wet and potentially cold. Those are ideal conditions in which many plants will rot, particularly cacti, succulents and other plants that grow in free-draining conditions.

A rule of thumb is that the plant should have an extra centimetre (½in) or so all the way around in the new pot and not a great deal more. If you are using a terracotta pot then it's very important that you wet the pot first, otherwise it wicks water away from the compost very quickly, sometimes stressing the plant out.

Turn your plant upside down, spreading your fingers across the top of the compost to take the weight of the plant, and then gently tap the edge of the pot and with luck the plant will slide out. If it's been in its pot for a while this may not happen – your first choice is to use an old kitchen knife and try and slide it around the inside of the pot, dislodging the roots that have stuck themselves to the side. If this doesn't work, you may have to break the pot. For this reason, I stay far away from any pot that has a narrower mouth than its width (anything goldfish-bowl shaped) because you almost always have to break these pots to get the plants out.

It's wise to have some newspaper or a tray to place your plant on once it's out of its old pot. It's a good idea at this point to take a look at the roots to make sure there are no pests or their eggs hiding, and to check their overall health.

Put a couple of centimetres (1in) or so of compost in the bottom of your new pot. It's not necessary to put crocks in the bottom of the pot; it's been proven that it really doesn't aid drainage in any way. However, it is sometimes worth putting a little square of plastic mesh over the drainage hole to stop the compost pouring out. If I don't have any mesh to hand I use a teabag; by the time it has broken down the compost will have settled into place and the roots will be starting to hold it together.

Place your plant in the pot and make sure it is sitting at the right height. If it sits proud above the top of the pot it will make watering a pain because it will nearly always cascade over the top. I like my plants to sit a centimetre or two below the rim. Gently nudge compost down around the sides of the plant, softly tapping the pot on its bottom so it settles. Do not force compost down the sides or overfirm it or you may damage the outside roots of the plant and you will compact the compost, leaving less room for the oxygen that the roots so desperately need.

The compost will settle and sink, particularly once it is watered. It may then be necessary to top dress the pot with more compost. It is important that the roots aren't exposed. You can also top dress with decorative mulch, polished pebbles or grit; this will help to deter compost

gnats. It will also help to lock in moisture and slow down evaporation and so conserve water.

Once you have potted up your plant, you can water it in. It's very important that you do this straight away after repotting, as dry compost will wick moisture away from the roots, which have just had a bit of a shock. Water the plant until you see it coming out of the bottom of the pot. It's easiest to do this in a sink and it's a good time to give the plant a shower and wash off any dust on the leaves or compost on the outside of a pot.

If you don't have a suitable space to do this, you can sit the pot in a tray of water until you see the top of the compost is moist. The dry compost will draw up the water naturally and this is a gentle way to ease the plant into its pot. Once the top is wet, sit the pot somewhere to drain. This is an ideal method to choose for plants that resent getting their foliage wet, such as cacti and carnivorous plants.

REPOTTING CACTI

Handling any cactus, even the seemingly gentle, furry Old Man cactus, could potentially make for a very painful repotting job. Those spines are designed to hurt and often it's not the obvious ones, but the tiny spine hairs that are the trickiest to pull out. I speak from experience. Donning big leather gloves is one option but you tend to break the spines and they won't grow back. The simplest trick is to use a long strip of newspaper. You want several pages to create a thick enough band that you can wrap around the cactus like a scarf, using the spare bit of paper as a handle. Then you can lift the cactus and gently knock it out of its pot. Allow the compost to dry out a bit before you do this as wet soil is heavy and will crumble quickly once out of the pot and damage the roots.

FEEDING YOUR HOUSEPLANTS

Your houseplants may arrive with slow-release fertiliser, often yellow or blue balls added to the compost, that breaks down slowly over time to give your plants nutrients. Usually this sort of slow-release fertiliser lasts for about six months, after that it is up to you. When the roots get potbound they cannot go in search of new nutrients so repotting a plant in new compost is one way to ensure plenty of new nutrition. Invest in good-quality, peat-free houseplant compost and it will be formulated to do the job for another six months or so. However, it is not always necessary or ideal to repot, and some fast-growing plants will exhaust the initial reserves in half that time so will need feeding. Most plants only need feeding while they are in full growth, usually from spring through to summer. In their down time they will need much less, just once a month is usually adequate.

Numerous manufactured liquid feeds are available, usually diluted with water and used every week or two weeks through the growing season. The compost should be moist before you add a liquid feed otherwise delicate young root hairs can be burnt by the application.

Some liquid feeds can be used as fast-acting foliar feeds. Here the feed is diluted with water and sprayed onto the foliage, where the leaves instantly absorb the nutrients.

Slow-release feeds usually take two to three weeks to become available to the plants. Whatever feed you use, make sure you follow the manufacturer's recommendations and never use more than is advised or more frequently. Too many nutrients can do more harm than good.

I like to use slow-release organic feed containing a mixture of organic plant nutrients and essential natural micro-organisms that improve root growth. It takes the hassle away from remembering to feed regularly. I just scatter the pellets on top of the compost and they slowly break down. I generally set a reminder on my phone throughout the growing season to make sure I remember when to feed any container plants.

KEEP THEIR ENEMIES AT BAY

On the whole, indoor plants don't suffer quite so badly from pests as their outdoor compatriots. This isn't to say there aren't a lot of things that want to eat them – and if pests do appear then an infestation can spread quickly because of the warmer conditions and few, if any, natural predators. But houseplants tend to not get as many pests for two reasons. Firstly, there aren't many of them in the same place. Once a pest has moved onto your plant it may decimate it, but your other houseplants are from such different places that they might not be on the critter's menu. But the chief reason why your houseplant doesn't get many pests is because it has probably been treated with a pesticide. Nobody has to tell you this, unless it's something you might decide to eat, like a lemon tree, in which case they will tell you not to eat it, rather than tell you what's been put on it.

Many of the pesticides growers use are systemic which usually means they are used as root drenches in the soil and the plant takes them up over a period of time. It's quite common that you have a plant for a number of years and it seems happily free from any pests and then bam, just like that, it gets an infestation. This is because the pesticide is no longer in the system. Systemic pesticides last anywhere from six months to five years.

No pesticide is good for the environment; many pesticides have dubious histories and increasingly we are finding out they aren't good for us. They certainly aren't good for insects and too often they can't discriminate between the good guys and the bad, which is why our bees are doing so badly around the world.

There are a few producers who grow houseplants without pesticides. They tend to be smaller, independent growers, the sort you'd find at farmers' markets. Some big companies like Walmart and Homebase have been pressured by consumers to stop using certain pesticides such as neonicitinoids, but

there's a whole suit of them that we never hear anything about. For this reason, you shouldn't add your dead houseplants to your compost because the pesticides will linger in your soil outside.

There are too many things to protest about these days and adding houseplants to your list may seems a step too far, but telling retailers, particularly the big guns, hardware and home stores that you'd prefer your plants to be pesticide free (and while we're on the subject, not grown in peat) is very important. The more you write, tell them at the store, tweet them and shout about things, the more they'll listen. They want your pennies at the end of the day.

All of the pests that will attack your houseplants can be dealt with by natural means and you should never need to resort to manufactured pesticides. The main culprits are aphids, soft scale, mealybugs, red spider mite and the occasional slug that manages to creep into your house.

Healthy houseplants can take on pests and win the battle. Underwatered, overwatered, underfed or overfed, unhappy plants, whatever their neglect, all suffer and become weak. So the first rule of pest defence is to keep your plants in good cheer. Water as regularly as the plant needs, water consistently, give the plant the conditions it likes and make sure that it has enough food to grow and you'll find you have few problems. Overfeeding your plant will make for soft, weak growth that is particularly susceptible to sap suckers, such as aphids, white fly and scale insects.

Regularly inspect your plants, turn them around and peer into their hidden spots to make sure all is good. If you do find you have the beginnings of an infestation, dislodge the pests. A good blast of lukewarm water from a shower will extricate a great many pests. Wash under the rim of the pot and inspect the bottom as these are favoured hiding holes.

Scale insects that look like tiny, orange-coloured-

Spots or patches of brown or yellow often indicate a lack of nutrients or scorching or water left on the leaves in sunlight.

Greenfly/aphids are best blasted off with strong water from the tap.

Powdery mildew is often caused by dryness and not enough air circulation.

Mealy bug can be destroyed with alcohol such as vodka or methylated spirits – use a paintbrush to dab onto the insect. Heavily infested planted should be composted.

Brown spots could be rust or, if at the edges, a sign that plants are overfed or underwatered. Rotting of the leaves or stem is often a sign of disease.

Red spider mite thrives in a dry atmosphere, so mist the leaves regularly and use a biological control.

Scale are small and immobile. They have a waxy shell and cling to the plant. Destroy them with alcohol or a biological control.

Grey mould is often caused by too much humidity in winter or when the plant has been kept too wet. Cut off infected leaves and bin.

Yellowing leaves with remain on the plant is often a sign of too much lime in the compost for lime-hating plants (such as carnivorous ones). If the leaves drop off, it is a sign of overwatering.

Blackfly/aphids are best blasted or washed off with a strong jet of water from the tap. If you see ladybirds near by, leave them to the job of destroying them.

Whitefly are tiny white, moth-like creatures that suck sap. Hard to get rid off, but biological controls *Encarsia* is very effective.

Leaf fall – shedding of older leaves is a sign of under-watering.

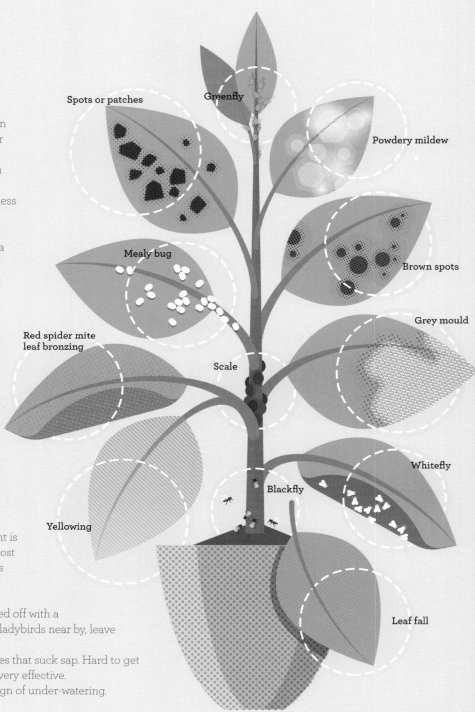

Spots or patches

Greenfly

Powdery mildew

Mealy bug

Brown spots

Grey mould

Red spider mite leaf bronzing

Scale

Whitefly

Blackfly

Yellowing

Leaf fall

blisters tend to stick to a few places. They love the midrib of the leaf, the underside, and in the cracks between the leaf stalk and the stem. The leaves will become sticky with their poo.

You can flick them off with your thumb, though this takes rather a long time, or you can dip a small paintbrush in vodka or high-proof alcohol and paint the insect – this will damage its waxy protective layer and kill it. Vodka does pretty well on mealybugs too, but they tend to move around bit more. Mealybugs look a bit like woodlice wearing a sheep's fleece.

Red spider mite is very hard to spot without a hand-lens because the spiders are tiny. The damage they do is very distinct. The top of the foliage will become pale and mottled and if you look very closely at the underside you'll see a fine webbing that covers the leaf and lots of small, two-spotted red mites moving around. The mottled colouring on the surface of the leaf is where they have been sucking sap. Red spider mites can only live in hot, dry conditions, which is why they can be so happy on our windowsills and in conservatories. The quickest way to deter them is to make the condition more humid, wet even. Take the plant to the shower and give it a good wash. Then mist it as many times a day as you can remember to. Sit the plant in a tray with pebbles and keep the tray full of water, as this will also boost humidity.

However, when you find serious numbers of any of these pests, dislodging them alone would keep you in a full-time job. When this happens it makes sense to use biological pest control. Australian ladybird larvae, *Cryptolaemus montrouzieri,* will eat mealybug. Soft scale is attacked by a parasitic wasp. Red spider mite is attacked by an even redder mite called *Phytoseiulus persimilis*. The parasitic wasp *Encarsia formosa* is very fond of turning whitefly into ghosts. A gang of tiny mites, *Aphidius praon* and *Aphidoletes aphidimyza,* will all happily munch on aphids.

Compost gnats or sciarid flies are small, black flies that lay their eggs in the surface of compost and other rotting organic matter. The larvae are tiny, almost see-through maggots that eat rotting organic matter, including plants that have been killed from overwatering. Although they rarely kill a plant, they can eat the roots of young seedlings and are generally a bit annoying to have flying around a plant. They need moist conditions to lay their eggs and one of the easiest ways to deter them is to make the surface of the compost less appealing. Grit, gravel, vermiculite or decorative pebbles over the top of the compost work very well. Otherwise you can source the biological control *Bacillus thuringiensis*, often sold as a liquid, that can be drenched into the compost and is very effective.

Your biological control will be sent in the post and they are live so it's important you don't leave them sitting in the sorting office. They usually come as eggs, sometimes as larval stage, in a little bottle or sometimes on squares of cardboard that you hang in your plants. They will come with instructions to keep the plant at a certain temperature or humidity; stick to these and nature will take care of the rest.

Fungis such as powdery mildews, damping off and botrytis can all be a problem on houseplants. They are nearly all made worse by inadequate watering and poor ventilation.

Pick off any diseased material and dispose of it in the bin and give the plants a little more room to breathe; open the window if the weather allows. Poke holes into the compost with a chopstick or similar object to get more oxygen to the roots and make sure the pots and containers are cleaned, particularly under the rims where all sorts of sins can fester.

MAKE BABIES: EASY PROPAGATION

Many of your houseplants are very easy to propagate. In fact, they are so desperate to do so that they often do the hard work for you. Think of spider plants with all those hanging baby spiders just waiting to touch a bit of soil and send down roots.

Other plants can easily be divided, just like outdoor growing plants. Offsets, runners and suckers are another straightforward way of creating new plants. Many plants can be rooted from cuttings, though this method does need more attention to get a good healthy root system.

DIVISION

Division is very simple, but cannot be done to plants that have a single stem, such as a climber, or plants that have leaves that arise from a single stem or rosette. When you are dividing, you are splitting stems and some roots from plants that form clumps or tufts to make new plants. If there's a single stem you just can't snap it in half. You cannot divide a money plant, *Crassula argentea,* for instance.

Dividing or splitting is easy, but sometimes it is very brutal. Even if a plant may be suitable for division, ripping it in half is destructive and only robust, strong-growing plants can usually tolerate it. But dividing plants can offer them a new lease of life. If the older parts are in the middle, for instance, division will allow the young, healthier growth room to grow.

The rule is that evergreen plants are best divided in spring, giving them plenty of time to recover because growth is active. Flowering plants should not be divided until after they have bloomed and there is a new flush of leaves growing.

Dividing is very messy. If you have to do it inside, spread out newspaper to contain the mess and have a sharp, clean knife to hand, with clean plant pots, potting

compost and somewhere you can water the plants in.

Remove the plant from the pot and lay it on its side. In order to split the plant successfully, each new division will need shoots and roots. You do not want to oversplit the plant; small divisions will have a hard time establishing themselves and often look a little ridiculous. Aim to divide a plant in half or perhaps into thirds at most.

You may need to use a sharp knife to cut between the roots; sometimes you can gently tease them apart. The aim is to break as few roots as possible. You could wash all the compost off the roots and tease them apart this way, but it's a very disruptive process to the most tender young roots. But if something is very hard to split, it's not a bad method.

Once you have your divisions, repot them into new pots, gently tapping new compost around the roots and then watering them in. It is very important that you keep your divisions somewhere shaded until they perk up. Some plants will flop about as they go through transplant shock and the roots adapt to their new world. Don't overwater them at this stage as you can easily drown a plant. A fine mist of water will help to keep transpiration down, which is usually why new divisions look so sad as the leaves are drawing up more water than roots can currently sup up. For this reason, your divisions should be roughly equal proportions of roots to leaves. More top growth than roots will mean transplantation shock is likely.

Plants that are easily increased by division include *Adiantum, Aechmea, Asparagus* species, *Aspidistra elatior, Calathea, Fittonia, Guzmania, Maranta, Spathiphyllum* and *Chlorophytum*.

SUCKERS, OFFSHOOTS AND RUNNERS

Plants that produce suckers, such as the Chinese money plant, *Peperomia*, are easy to propagate, but the suckers must be a reasonable size so they are easy to handle. Knock the plant out of the pot and gently disentangle the roots of the young plant from that of the mother plant. You have to break a few roots along the way, but it's usually obvious how to do it.

Plants that grow offsets on runners, like the spider plant, are also easy to deal with. The offsets should have roots or the beginning of them and again be large enough to handle. You have two choices: you can either cut off the young offset and repot it. Or you can pin the young offset with wire (you can unravel a paper clip) into a new pot of compost. When the new plant is growing well, cut off the runner.

Bromeliads often produce pups or baby offsets around the mother plant, particularly after it has flowered. Cut down the flower spike as it begins to wither and usually the mother plant will start to die back, leaving the offsets to continue to grow. You can just leave the plant, removing the mother plant when the offsets are ready to be pulled away, but the new offsets often look lopsided in the pot so it is better to remove the plant from the pot, cut off the offsets and repot. You will need a sharp knife to cut the pups away from the thick, woody root of the mother plant, but it's easy enough to distinguish one from the other.

STEM PROPAGATION

Many of your houseplants have been raised from cuttings. You can do the same – some are so easy they need to do no more than sit in a glass of water while others are fiendishly difficult. Vines and climbers that never stop flowering often don't provide enough suitable material to propagate from, others need bottom heat and must root in 80 per cent humidity and sterile conditions. Start with some easy ones that are fun to propagate.

Begonias, *Tradescantia*, ivy, pelargoniums, lemon grass, mint and *Calathea* can all be easily rooted in a glass of water. As the cutting sits in the water it releases its own rooting hormones to encourage the buds on the stem that are sitting in water to become roots. For this reason, you don't want a huge glass of water because the rooting hormone is too dilute and it takes ages for new roots to appear. Once the roots are several centimetres long, simply pot the cutting into compost. The compost should be kept moist, but not waterlogged, until the plant starts to grow.

Your cutting should be anywhere from 10–20cm (4–8in) long, cut off cleanly just below a joint or bud in the stem. Remove the leaves from the lower part of the stem that will sit in water and place the stem in your glass of water. Rooting should happen within 2–3 weeks, though for something like rosemary with a woody stem this make take longer. It's best to take these sorts of cutting in spring and summer when active growth is happening.

Some plants love to root in water, others hate it and the success rate is very low, particularly when you transplant the cutting from water to compost. For this

reason it makes more sense to start many cuttings off in compost. The cuttings are treated exactly the same way, though you can dip the end in root hormone (bought from a good garden centre), which speeds things along.

Fill a 15cm (6in) pot with potting compost into which you've mixed some horticultural sand, grit or vermiculite. The compost needs to be open and airy for successful rooting. Using a pencil or chopstick, make a hole for the cutting and push it in. On the whole, cuttings prefer to be placed around the edge of the pot rather than the middle. I guess it must have something to do with drainage, but it's as if they prefer the comfort of an edge and to be tucked in rather than sitting in the middle of the pot. In a 15cm (6in) diameter pot you can get three or four 10cm (4in) cuttings. You need to keep the pot out of direct sunlight as cuttings will die very quickly if they get too hot. Ideally you want to keep humidity very high around the cuttings so they don't lose water. One way to do this is to cover the pot with a clear plastic bag so that the cuttings are in a miniature greenhouse. You may have to fashion some wire or chopsticks around the pot to hold the bag off the leaves of the cuttings.

PROPAGATING FROM ADVENTITIOUS ROOTS

Many houseplants will produce adventitious roots on their stems. This is them telling you they are ready for some new ground. Hoyas and a number of succulents do this regularly. You have two choices here: you can either cut off a length of stem with roots (in the hoya's case they don't look like roots, but are visible bumps) and propagate as a cutting. Or you can pin them down into fresh compost so that they actively start to grow and then remove the offset from the mother plant. For hoyas, I think it makes most sense to propagate the adventitious roots in compost while still attached and cut the stem off to make a new plant when you see signs of new growth. For succulents, it often makes more sense to take the roots/cutting off the plant and repot it.

LEAF CUTTINGS

Many cacti and succulents are easy to propagate from cuttings. You need to do this from late spring to midsummer for the best results with cacti and in early spring or late summer for succulents.

How the cutting is taken depends a little on the genus. If they have pads, such as a barrel-shaped cactus, you slice or break off a pad, and with something like a Christmas cactus you take the cutting at a joint. The cutting then has to dry out and callus over for two days, just leave it resting by the plant. Once you can see the end has callused over (and it's very obvious) you can plant the cutting in a small plastic pot filled with one part compost to one part coarse sand. The compost should be moist but not wet as this will rot the cuttings. Push the cutting in to about 1cm (½in) and place the cuttings somewhere warm but out of direct light. It will either work or not within ten days. Bottom heat from an electrical propagator will make a huge difference but isn't strictly necessary.

Many succulents propagate from leaf cuttings. Often you don't even have to do anything as the leaves fall off, callus over and start rooting in whatever pot they've fallen into. If you've seen an *Echeveria* at a friends that you're madly in love with or want a new money plant, you just have to get hold of a single leaf. Choose a ripe, plump leaf that is not too young and carefully pull it from the plant. Leave it to callus over for two days and then lay it on top of a small pot with compost mixed to the ratio one part compost to two parts coarse sand or grit. Gently nudge the leaf end barely into the compost and you can top dress with grit around it. Water the leaf in and don't water again until you see signs of life. The first of these will be tiny, baby leaves at the end of the leaf. It will take a while for these plants to grow into substantial houseplants, but it's so much fun propagating that you'll find yourself doing it endlessly (or at least I do).

Many houseplants can be propagated merely from a leaf. Begonias, particularly *Begonia rex, Sansevieria trifasciata* (mother-in-law's tongue), *Streptocarpus* and *Saintpaulia* are all easily rooted from leaf cuttings.

Begonias in particular can be rooted from parts of a leaf or a whole leaf – 2cm (1in) long pieces of leaf can be laid flat on damp sand and pegged down with wire loops inserted into the middle of the leaf so that the leaf is in close contact with the sand. Plantlets will grow where the cuts have been made, if there is enough moisture and warmth, so it makes sense to put the pot in a clear bag so that growing conditions remain moist.

The same thing can be done with a whole leaf, pegging it down so that it is is in close contact with the sand. Rooting can take several weeks, so be patient and don't water the sand, just keep the conditions humid. As the plantlets appear, gradually open up the bag allowing more air and lowering the temperature so that the plantlets start to harden off. When they have two or three good leaves they are ready to be put into individual pots (the mother leaf will start to die back). The plantlets must be kept in a humid environment for around another three weeks then can be treated as you would normally treat a begonia.

Sansevieria trifasciata (mother-in-law's tongue) can be propagated by leaf cuttings or divisions (pictured on page 27). Leaf cuttings are best done in spring or summer. Choose a healthy leaf away from the central crown and slice it off, then, cutting across the leaf, slice it into 5cm (2in) sections. Cut a tiny triangle out of the bottom edge of each cutting as they must all be propagated in the direction they were growing and not upside down. Push the cuttings with the snipped end down into a pot with good-quality potting compost. After about six weeks a new young plant will develop from each cutting. The compost must be damp when you insert the cuttings, but don't overwater until you see new signs of growth or else the cuttings will rot off. Conversely, don't let the compost completely dry out either. For some curious reason, the cuttings will be mottled green and white and won't show the striped variegation of the parent.

LATIN NAMES

Latin names are sometimes long and complicated, often difficult to pronounce and baffling to spell, but they do mean that we are all on the same page. Many plants have numerous common names and sometimes a number of genera share the same common name. Latin names also cross language barriers and mean that we can all talk plants wherever we come from.

The great grandfather of naming, Linnaeus, came up with our universal language for all living things, known as the binomial system. Here everything living belongs to a family, and has a surname and a first name. Latin names should be italicised and the species name should always be lower case. To confuse things further, many Latin names are actually derived from Greek, Arabic or German.

Sometimes species names are very common. For example, *japonica* is used for many plants that came from Asia, often nowhere near Japan. *Pumila* means dwarf, *alba* means white, *saggitaria* means shield-shaped and on and on and on. There are whole dictionaries that allow you to decipher how, when and why plants are named as they are. If the history or root of the name is interesting or informative, I've included it, mostly because I am a geek when it comes to this sort of thing. And partly to make up for that day-long lecture and thousand-word essay on the importance of the binomial system and Latin names I endured at Kew.

All names are written in this order: genus, species, family. The genus is the surname; the species is the first name. The Swiss cheese plant is known as *Monstera* (genus) *deliciosa* (species) and it comes from a large tropical family known as Araceae. All family names end in 'aceae' (pronounced A-C-eee).

Many plants have further suffixes to their name to distinguish cultivars, varieties, forms and subspecies. Cultivars are always bred from cultivation, by humans, and are not italicised but written in single inverted commas. Varieties can be bred or naturally occurring and are distinguished by the abbreviation 'var'. in front of the name. If it's naturally occurring from the wild, then it is written as, for example, *Fittonia verschaffeltii* var. *argyroneura*. If it is bred, then it is put in inverted commas – for example, *Peperomia caperata* 'Variegata'. At some point, someone decided to get snooty about the whole thing and varieties are no longer to be Latinised. Subspecies are recognisably different taxonomically from the species, but not so different they require a new species. Subspecies are abbreviated to 'subsp'. 'Forms' or 'forma' refer to a morphological form – usually a different flower colour – that occurs naturally and is then selected to breed from.

Plants that like...

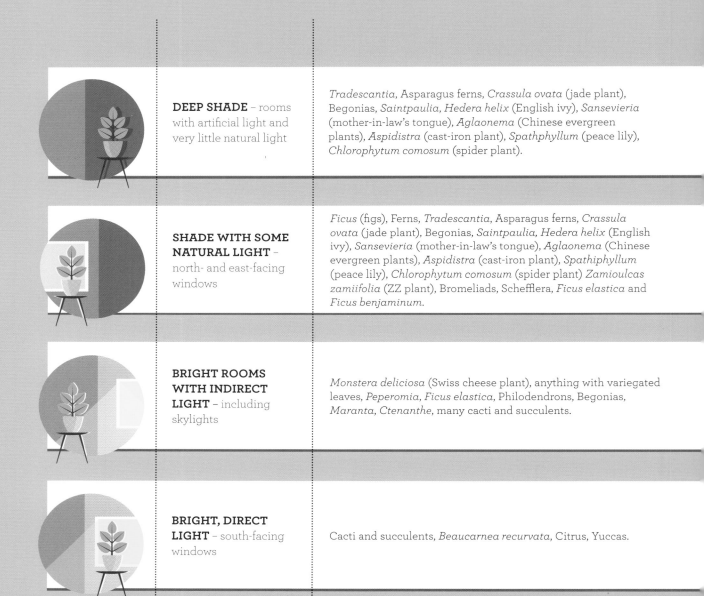

DEEP SHADE – rooms with artificial light and very little natural light

Tradescantia, Asparagus ferns, *Crassula ovata* (jade plant), Begonias, *Saintpaulia*, *Hedera helix* (English ivy), *Sansevieria* (mother-in-law's tongue), *Aglaonema* (Chinese evergreen plants), *Aspidistra* (cast-iron plant), *Spathphyllum* (peace lily), *Chlorophytum comosum* (spider plant).

SHADE WITH SOME NATURAL LIGHT – north- and east-facing windows

Ficus (figs), Ferns, *Tradescantia*, Asparagus ferns, *Crassula ovata* (jade plant), Begonias, *Saintpaulia*, *Hedera helix* (English ivy), *Sansevieria* (mother-in-law's tongue), *Aglaonema* (Chinese evergreen plants), *Aspidistra* (cast-iron plant), *Spathiphyllum* (peace lily), *Chlorophytum comosum* (spider plant) *Zamioulcas zamiifolia* (ZZ plant), Bromeliads, Schefflera, *Ficus elastica* and *Ficus benjaminum*.

BRIGHT ROOMS WITH INDIRECT LIGHT – including skylights

Monstera deliciosa (Swiss cheese plant), anything with variegated leaves, *Peperomia*, *Ficus elastica*, Philodendrons, Begonias, *Maranta*, *Ctenanthe*, many cacti and succulents.

BRIGHT, DIRECT LIGHT – south-facing windows

Cacti and succulents, *Beaucarnea recurvata*, Citrus, Yuccas.

Hedera helix (English ivy), *Crassula ovata* (jade plant), Lemons, *Aspidistra* (cast-iron plant), *Cycas revoluta* (sago palm), Asparagus ferns, *Adiantum, Asplenium nidus* (bird's-nest fern), *Nephrolepsis, Pteris.*

COLD ROOMS WITH NO HEAT – porches, sunrooms

Thick-leaved fleshy plants do best in these conditions; think *Echeveria, Sedum, Agave*, cacti and succulents.

HOT ROOMS THAT GET VERY WARM – because of fires, cookers or just because you like it toasty

Sansevieria (mother-in-law's tongue), *Aloe vera*, Cacti, Succulents, *Chlorophytum comosum* (spider plant), *Philodendron*, Yuccas, *Zamioculcas zamiifolia*,(ZZ plant). Stay away from ferns, which hate dry atmospheres.

HEAT SOURCES – sometimes you have to put your plants very close to heat sources, in particular radiators that dry the atmosphere

Aechmea, Billbergia, Chlorophytum comosum, Clivia, Ficus elastica, Grevillea, Pilea, Sansevieria, Vriesea, Tradescantia, cacti and succulents.

HUMID – bathroom, kitchen sink

Edible plants

I can't help myself. I see a stray bit of life and my desire to give it love, soil and some water is instinctive, perhaps evolutionary; I am a gardener through and through. And everyone's fruit bowl is a potential garden in the making. Growing your leftover groceries into houseplants is no quick fix and is certainly unlikely to replenish your fruit bowl, but it is easy, free and a great solution for those on the endless renter's shuffle. Get them growing, enjoy them, leave them behind, start again.

AVOCADO

Perhaps the simplest of all grocery pips to get to germinate. You'll need a jar, some pins or toothpicks and a little patience. Fill the jar with water and stick 3 pins in your avocado pip so that it can hover with 2cm (1in) of the flat, bottom end sitting in the water. The pip does not need light to germinate, so you can keep it somewhere warm and dry (as long as you remember to check on it) until the first few roots appear. Once this happens, bring it somewhere light and warm and wait for the first shoot. The whole pip will split apart as this happens. Once the shoot is 10cm (4in) or so, pot it up into houseplant compost, giving the roots plenty of space to run. Avocados do not like to be root bound. Once the shoot has 3–4 leaves, nip out the growing tip to encourage the plant to branch out, otherwise you'll get a very spindly avocado. The more space you give avocados the more they will grow, so keep potting them on if you want big houseplants. They grow into considerable trees in the wild. Bright, direct light will scorch the leaves and plants will require a lot of watering to stay happy. They ideally want bright, indirect light with conditions around 15°C/60°F.

CITRUS FRUIT

Lemons, oranges, clementines, limes and grapefruit can all be grown from their pips, although the results

are variable and it will be at least 15 years before you see fruit and find out whether it tastes good or not! However, in that time you can use the lovely aromatic leaves in teas or simply boiled up in water to scent the house. The flowers smell divine and it's worth growing citrus for these alone.

You need ripe fruit for good germination; it should be soft and just beginning to go over. Remove the pips and wash them of any residue that might cause the seeds to go mouldy in the compost. In a small pot, plant 3–4 seeds, 1–2cm (less than 1in) below the compost level and water the pot. Citrus germinate at high temperatures, between 20–28°C/68–84°F and need moist conditions to succeed. Keep the pot on your warmest windowsill, or a heat propagator if you have such a thing. To make sure that the pot is continually moist, place it inside a clear plastic bag until germination occurs. This usually takes 2 weeks. Once the seedlings are up and have 3 leaves, you can prick them out into a larger pot. They need to be kept in bright, warm conditions, again making sure that the compost is moist, but not waterlogged.

Grapefruit make very sprawling plants, lemons can take the coolest conditions – down to 5°C/40°F – and limes need much warmer conditions, year-round above 15°C/60°F.

CHILLIES

If you taste a good chilli, it is always worth keeping a few of the seeds (not from anything cooked though as these seeds are denatured and won't germinate). Chillies germinate around 18–22°C/65–71°F. The hotter Thai chillies tend to need more heat and they can take a little longer to germinate. They need open compost for germination – if you can add some vermiculite then

do. Place the seeds 1cm (½in) below the compost so that the seeds are covered, and water in. Seal the pot in a clear plastic bag and keep it somewhere bright and warm. When the seedlings have 3 leaves, pot them on. Chillies are hungry plants and need to be regularly repotted when young. If you see the roots coming out of the drainage holes in the bottom of the pot, it's time to move up one size. Once you have the plant in its final pot, anywhere from 1 litre for small chilli plants to 10 litres for bigger ones, feed fortnightly with liquid feed, such as organic tomato feed, and you'll find you get a lot more chillies to harvest. You can pinch the plants out when they reach 10–15cm (4–6in) to encourage branching out and a more bushy appearance. Chillies can withstand a little drying out between watering, but don't ever want to be bone dry. Overwatering results in blander-flavoured chillies.

COFFEE

Coffee is a little more complicated. You will need to befriend a coffee roaster because a bean that has been jostling around at 200°C to make a brew sure isn't going to germinate. You need a fresh, green bean, and coffee roasters have plenty of those. Perhaps charm them with an offer of going halves on the ones that germinate.

Ask your coffee merchant for their most recent batch in; coffee remains viable for around 4 months, but fresh seed germinates much quicker. Four month old seed can take up to 6 months to germinate! First, you will need to soak the green beans for 24 hours to rehydrate them. There is some evidence that scarifying the seed speeds up germination. If you want to do this, rub the rounded end of the bean on some sandpaper so that you start to wear away the seed coat. The seed is best pre-germinated in wet sand or wet vermiculite. Coffee germinates at high temperatures, around 22–28°C/72–82°F, so it makes sense to cover the vermiculite/sand with a clear plastic bag, otherwise you'll constantly be topping up the moisture. Once the seed has germinated and you see the radicle (the first seedling root) appear, pot the seed into houseplant compost with the seed just 1–2cm (less than 1in) below the surface and keep the compost damp. Baby seedling leaves will appear fairly quickly, followed by the adult leaves. When the plant is 15–20cm (6–8in) high you can nip out the top to encourage branching.

Coffee needs about 4–5 hours of bright light a day to do well. It likes humid conditions, so sitting your plant in a saucer of pebbles and water will improve humidity, particularly if you have to keep the plant near a radiator to meet its temperature requirement. Coffee likes a daytime temperature between 18–26°C/65–78°F and a night temperature of around 10°C/50°F. Coffee flowers smell utterly heavenly, but the plant only tends to flower when it's at least 5 years old.

LEMON GRASS

This is best grown from shop-bought stems, which can be rooted in water easily. Lemon grass is actually a marginal water plant and the happiest pot-grown ones will sit in regularly-refreshed water throughout the summer. They love a warm, sunny position and will thrive on a south-facing windowsill. In winter, plants will need less water, but should never completely dry out. Often they go dormant. You probably won't get fat bulbs of lemon grass, but the leaves will be much more pungent than shop-bought stuff, so this hardly matters.

BASILS

Thai basil, or for that matter any other basil you care for, can be quickly and easily rooted in water. Choose healthy, firm stems, roughly 15–25cm (6–10in) long and remove the lower leaves so that there are no more than 3–4 leaves left per stem. Stick them in a clean jar of water and leave them on a bright, warm windowsill making sure that the water never completely evaporates. Within 2 weeks you should see roots, when these are roughly 2cm (1in) long, pot the stem, cutting individually into a 9cm pot or slightly larger, in houseplant compost or organic vegetable compost. Allow the compost to just about dry out between watering; if it stays too moist you will rot the plant. When the plant has put on new growth, you can pinch the growing tip out to encourage bushiness.

Eventually your plants will start to flower. Either enjoy the flowers and collect the seed (it's edible and can be

used to make basil drinks) for the next round, or take cuttings (from non-flowering shoots). Basil from seed is very easy, particularly for Italian green basil, but I find Thai basil is easier from cuttings. African blue basil is perennial and rarely sets seed, so has to be propagated by cuttings. If you can get hold of some, do. It makes perhaps the prettiest windowsill edible, flowering endlessly in the summer (no viable seed means it's on a perpetually, if useless, mission to try and set some) and tastes delicious. The flowers are purple-blue and the leaves have very pretty purple-blue midribs.

OTHER EDIBLES YOU CAN ROOT IN WATER

If rooting edibles works for you, then there are others you can try: watercress, water spinach, mint, tarragon (in spring, by summer it may rot off), and rosemary (spring cuttings do best in water; by summer, cuttings

need to be rooted in compost), all will root in water. Rosemary may take some time, and if the stem goes soft and rots, time to start again.

Sweet potatoes will also root in water. Suspend them like you would an avocado pip, this time with the flat, cut end pointing upwards. New shoots and roots will quickly appear. When the shoots are 10cm (4in) or so long, carefully twist them off and root them in water.

Once they have roots that are several centimetres long you can plant them up. In theory, you could plant the tuber, but in practise they often rot in the compost before they have sent out shoots. They will need very big containers to produce more sweet potatoes and are best grown as a greenhouse or hot courtyard crop because they need a lot of water. However, the leaves are very pretty and they make excellent trailing plants for your home.

Succulents

Succulents are a large group of plants that include cacti. The common theme in the group is the ability to store water in the leaves or stems so that they can survive in arid conditions. For this reason, succulents have plump, fat leaves. Succulents are often found growing in desert and savannah situations where there is little moisture, dry air and bright sunlight. The soil always has good drainage and the daytime temperatures are high. The difference between a succulent and cacti is the presence of areoles, specialised sites where spines form. Cacti have spines, succulents don't. Many succulents are grey or grey-blue in colour to reflect the intense light of the bright conditions they live in.

Succulents like well-open and free-draining compost similar to their natural habitat. This prevents waterlogging, which is the quickest way to kill a succulent. Add extra – up to 30 per cent extra – grit to houseplant compost to aid drainage. From early spring onwards, water succulents freely, allowing excess water to drain away. You can feed your succulents with a houseplant feed from from spring to early autumn, once a month. Succulents benefit from good air circulation, particularly during the summer months. From early autumn onwards, reduce watering to a minimum to encourage a rest period, allowing the compost to virtually dry out before watering again.

Aloe, Aloeceae

Aloe is another huge genus of succulent plants. There's one standout species, *Aloe vera*, that everyone knows about and then another 499 or so species that span tropical and southern Africa, Madagascar, Jordan, the Arab Peninsula and numerous small islands in the Indian Ocean. All aloes have thick fleshy leaves in rosette formation and the flowers are tubular, usually yellow, orange, pink or red in densely clustered pendants. Some aloes have no stem and the rosette grows directly from the ground; others have clambering stems and some are much more tree-like and have considerable branching stems.

Aloes are nearly always found growing in very free-draining, rocky places with low fertility. Those thick leaves are a defence against drying out and the blue-green, grey-green colouring is an adaption to strong radiation. This lot want to bake on a hot, sunny windowsill and won't be at all fazed by living next to a radiator. And they don't tend to care two hoots whether you repot them often or not. In short, these are very tough, undemanding plants. If and when you do decide to pot them in new compost, make sure it's very free-draining, adding at least 50 per cent grit, coarse sand or perlite to any shop-bought potting mix. Repot in late winter or spring, at best every 3–4 years.

You can move your aloes outside in summer months; they hugely benefit from good air circulation. During the growing season, water them by drenching the pot and then only watering again when the pot has almost dried out; and give them a liquid feed every once in a while. Over the winter, watering can drop down to about once a month; the soil should not be completely arid, but it can go pretty near there. Make sure they have a minimum temperature between 6-10°C/42-50°F at night and all will be good in their world.

Various aloes have been used medicinally for a very long time. They appear in early Greek text and both the Greeks and Romans used *Aloe vera* to treat wounds. It's particularly good for burns and the unprocessed insides of the leaves is a known laxative (just a warning if you decide to juice them). The name *Aloe* is derived from the Arab, *alloch* or from *allal*, meaning bitter, suggesting how long it has been used to aid digestion.

The larger species of *Aloe* are not really suitable houseplants, but some of the smaller ones are very attractive and pretty hard to kill. Every kitchen should have an *Aloe vera* plant for minor burns alone.

Aloe aristata, **Lace aloe** is a popular species. The dark green leaves are dotted with white warts and the margins gently saw-toothed, with each leaf ending in a thread-like tip. It looks a lot fiercer than it is and it forms very dense rosettes that eventually make clumps as it likes to offset regularly. It comes from South Africa and Lesotho, where is spans dry, sandy regions, mountainsides and shady, forested valleys, but always in very free-draining soils. This one can withstand both a sunny windowsill and a relatively shady position and doesn't even mind the odd cold night. The tubular orange flowers are very rich in nectar and in their native habitat visited by birds, bees and wasps. The offsets can be separated and pot on easily, so you'll find you have plenty to give away.

Aloe arborescens, **Kranz aloe**, is the super cousin of *Aloe vera*; its juice is known to be full of health benefits. It's also much bigger and needs a large pot to be happy, but if you have the space, a light stairwell or such, then it's well worth growing. It is a large multi-headed, sprawling thing that can reach tree size. It has blue-green leaves that are toothed along the margins. The flowers are bright orange-red and rather spectacular, usually appearing in late winter.

Aloe burgersfortensis is harder to get hold of, but well worth it. The leaves are very dark, greyish-purple, red-brown and are long and thick. This one likes to fling its arms wide of the pot which can make it a tricky one to grow on a windowsill. It has attractive white markings that

run down the length of the leaves like a series of stretched dots. The more sun you give this one the more reddish-brown it turns in colour.

Aloe variegata, **Tiger aloe, Partridge-breasted aloe**, is native to South Africa and Namibia. It gets its common name from its tiger stripes of rich green with irregular pale green stripes. The leaves are arranged in 3 ranks and new leaves appear individually over time from the centre of the plant. The flowers are reddish in colour and appear once the plant is mature. It grows in very rocky terrain where it crouches between boulders that offer shade from the harsh midday sun. Don't be fooled into thinking it wants shade in your house, though; it will do best in full sun.

Aloe vera (pictured) forms a dense rosette of rather thick, grey-green, often tinged red leaves with toothed, pale margins. Younger leaves are often spotted. This one likes to sucker, so you get lots of offshoots to pot up if you want to go into cosmetics or juicing (see the warning opposite about its laxative effect).

Haworthia, Asphodelaceae

Haworthia is a large genus very closely related to aloes, although they tend to be much smaller and flower differently. They are rosette forming, mostly stemless with tough, firm fleshy leaves that are usually dark green. Some contain epidermal windows to allow sunlight to filter in to help photosynthesis. All are endemic to South Africa, Swaziland, Namibia and Mozambique, where they are found growing in bright light – but not full sun – in rocky and desert-like conditions. Water generously in the summer, allowing the plant to dry out between waterings. In winter, water every other month. Despite being plants from arid regions, they do like some shade and full sun will upset them.

Haworthia attenuata, **Zebra plant**, has tapered leaves with bands of white markings along them. It is clump forming, produces many offsets and is a tough and undemanding houseplant.

Haworthia cuspidata is a hybrid between two species. It forms a star-like rosette, though in time will form a clump as offsets are produced. The leaves are wedge-shaped, lime green to grey-green with prominent windows of translucent areas near the tips. The flowers are white.

Haworthia fasciata is so similar looking to *H. attenuata* that the two are often mistaken. The difference is the white markings are only on the underside of the leaf, and the leaves are slightly shorter and slightly fatter.

Haworthia limifolia is native to southern Africa, and grows up to 10cm (4in) tall. The leaves are triangular to ovate, spreading broad at the base. It has prominent white markings along the leaf. 'Spider White' (pictured) has wavy white markings along the base.

Haworthia margaritifera, **Pearl bearer**, is clump forming and produces masses of offsets. Each leaf is olive green, but can blush red if stressed or cold. Tiny, greenish-white bumps resembling pearls cover the outer side of the leaves, hence its name.

Aeonium,
Crassulaceae

There is something so very satisfying about aeoniums; their dense, flat rosettes of leathery leaves make for such pleasing houseplant arrangements. Aeoniums are native to the Canary Islands and Mediterranean areas such as Portugal, Spain, Sicily, Morocco, Sardinia and to East Africa. They thrive in hot, harsh, rocky places, where their thick succulent leaves can weather the heat. When conditions get really tough, they go dormant – in midsummer and sometimes in winter.

The name comes from the Greek *aionos,* often translated as 'ageless', but also refers to anything that is enduring or durable or everlasting, which is a more accurate description of how they get through very hot summers.

There are around 35 species of aeoniums. All of them are frost tender and vary wildly in size from tiny, almost flat discs to more woody shrubs with stout stems supporting one or more disc-shaped rosettes. The rosette elongates when the plant is about to flower. The flowers are panicles of many small yellow or white flowers. The leaves are definitely the crowning glory of this plant. Aeoniums naturally hybridise which means there are many cultivars out there. If you like aeoniums and they like you, it's well worth becoming a collector.

As they like rocky places, aeoniums must be grown in free-draining, gritty compost and must be kept in full sun. They will sulk if left in the shade. If the conditions get too cool in the winter (and they must remain frost free) they will drop their leaves, but these will soon be replaced in spring. Aeoniums prefer a minimum temperature of 6°C/42°F. They need to be watered throughout the year, but from November to February water very sparingly. During their growing period from late spring to summer they should be fed once a month.

Many aeoniums are monocarpic, which means once they flower they die. However, non-flowering offsets will survive but these may give you a very strange-looking plant. Instead of persevering with a strange beast, propagate the rosettes that remain. To do this, cut the rosette off with about 2cm (1in) of basal stem below the leaf. Set the rosette on its side on a saucer so that the basal stem starts to dry off and heal over; this will take a few days. Then pot the rosette up in gritty compost and water very sparingly. Eventually new roots will form and you can tell this is happening because new leaves will appear in the centre of the rosette. This way you can perpetually keep aeoniums living up to their name.

Aeonium arboreum, **Tree houseleek** (pictured), can grow up to 60cm (2ft) tall, with tree-like stems that branch and end with a rosette of bright green, shiny leaves. In winter or early spring, panicles of tiny yellow flowers often appear. The cultivar *Aeonium arboreum* 'Schwartzkopf' ('Zwartkop') is perhaps most popular because you get almost black leaves, which makes for a very striking plant. *Aeonium arboretum* 'Afrofuturism' has purple leaves that often flush green in spring before turning to their summer colours.

Aeonium tabuliforme comes from Tenerife where it is mainly found growing on cliffs and has very tight, flat, wide geometric rosettes. By its third year, these rise into a dome and flower, at which point the plant dies. You can sometimes stave this off by keeping it in slightly shadier conditions, but in the end once it decides it needs to flower there's little you can do. Let the flower spike set seed and dry then scatter the seeds onto compost. Even if you do this around the dying plant, more often than not these seeds

will germinate. *A. tabuliforme* will also readily germinate from leaves; just pull a leaf off, let it callus over and then rest it on compost – you'll find it quickly sends out new pink roots. The densely packed rosettes of the plant often cover the entire pot and it's very important that you don't get water on them as the leaves will damage if water settles. Water from below instead.

***Aeonium haworthii*, Pinwheel aeonium**, comes from the Canary Isles. It has numerous branching stems each with a rosette of blueish-green leaves often tinged with red margins. Flowers appear in late spring and are very pale yellow to almost white. Keep this one almost completely dry over winter until spring when growth starts up again, and feed it over summer. Again, if you want to take cuttings, let them callus over and then keep them barely moist until rooted.

Echeveria, Crassulaceae

Echeveria is another group of rosette-forming succulents – plumper, fuller American cousins to aeoniums, if you like. They are mostly found in semi-desert areas of central and southern America, with many coming from Mexico. They get their name from the eighteenth-century Mexican botanical artist Atanasio Echeverria y Godoy.

It's a very large genus; there are around 150 species and many more cultivars with a great deal of variety within the basic rosette formation. Thin leaves, crinkled leaves, fat leaves, hairy leaves, brightly coloured leaves and every variation in between means that they have always been highly valued as collector's plants. The leaf colour often gets more pronounced in cold weather and can withstand very light frosts, making them an excellent choice if you live in a cold garret or icy studio.

Echeverias can be evergreen or deciduous, though most of the common houseplants are evergreen types.

They like the same temperature as aeoniums, needing a minimum of 6°C/42°F to grow. Most are summer growers and once established they can withstand extended droughts, which makes them an excellent choice if you're a neglectful waterer, or if they are somewhere you're just not going to get to water them often, very high windowsills for instance. They can easily survive being watered every two weeks or so. Saying that, the healthiest, finest-looking specimens are not neglected, and they are best watered year-round, although in winter this should be very sparingly, just so the compost never completely dries out. They require less fertiliser than aeoniums and need only be fed a couple of times during the growing season.

These are plants that grow in very free-draining soils in their desert conditions and in your home they need to be grown in sunny conditions to do well. Dull conditions will cause the rosette to elongate and the colours to fade. They have shallow roots that make the most of the limited amounts of organic debris that you find in desert conditions. This means that the roots are very liable to rot off if they sit in water or the compost is too heavy. If in doubt, repot the plant with 50 per cent grit to achieve better drainage. Too often these plants are grown in peat-heavy compost that is liable to swing from bone dry to sodden if you're an erratic waterer and this is not fun for the poor echeveria.

Echeverias are polymorphic meaning that they flower and set seed freely over their life time. Often when they flower the neat, compact rosette elongates to make room for the flower spike. The flowers range from orange to pink and are a pretty bell shape, so personally I like it when they appear, but you can chop them off as you see the spike emerging to keep the plant a more compact shape, though once something decides it wants to flower this can be a slightly futile job. If kept in poor light conditions the rosette will elongate to stretch to its light source.

Like many of these rosette-forming plants, after a number of years they start to grow a little tall and gangly and lose their lower leaves, which slightly spoils the perfect compact rosette that people yearn for. You can propagate them by cutting off the rosette with an inch or so of stem and re-rooting in free-draining compost, watering very sparingly until the roots appear. Personally, I like their eccentric older selves and think that forcing them to be forever youthful is a little harsh; allow them to age gracefully.

48

Echeveria affinis comes from western Mexico and with time will form solid mounds of many rosettes. Each rosette is lime green, often fringed with a red-brown edge. It has particularly pretty flowers in summer that are pink on the outside opening to creamy white petals. There are numerous near black to dark red forms and cultivars that are worth looking out for.

Echeveria agavoides has a very short stem and often makes a solitary rosette. The leaves are deep green, waxy with transparent margins. The flowers appear in spring to early summer and are pink-orange on the outside and yellow within. There are numerous cultivars with red margins or red tips. A fairly rare, but strange cultivar called 'Carnunculata' has warty excretions over the leaves, not pretty, but interesting.

Echeveria albicans, **Whitening echeveria**, has very plump, palest blue-green leaves forming packed rosettes that quickly form dense clumps. In spring it produces small coral pink flowers with yellow centres.

Echeveria **'Doris Taylor'** is hairy, deliciously so, with pale grey hairs over blue-green foliage. You'll want to stroke it.

Echeveria elegans, **Mexican snowball, white Mexican rose** or **Mexican gem** (pictured) is from, you've guessed it, Mexico. It has a short stem and lovely rosettes of thick, blue-green concave leaves with distinct pointed tips. With time it forms numerous offsets. The flowers are pink on the outside, yellow-orange within.

Echeveria harmsii is an upright plant on short stems that branch and terminate in a rosette. The leaves are hairy, narrow, dark green with pronounced red margins, as if it has dipped itself in raspberry jam. It's a strange-looking thing, but tactile and pleasing.

Echeveria secunda **var.** *glauca* forms dense clumps of blue-grey rosettes with pale, crisp margins and tips. It has spikes of bright red flowers in summer.

Echeveria setosa, **Mexican firecracker**, has very beautiful soft, dense, white hairs all over the leaves that glow in bright light. From late spring, it has red and yellow flowers, though it's the hairs that make this one irresistible.

SPRING　SUMMER　AUTUMN　WINTER

Sedum, Stonecrops, Crassulaceae

Stonecrops are leafy succulents primarily found in the northern hemisphere, though there are some great southern hemisphere ones that make wonderful houseplants.

Sedum morganianum, Donkey tail, is my favourite sedum and is native to southern Mexico and Honduras. It has long, trailing stems that can grow up to 60cm (2ft) with fleshy, blue-green leaves. 'Burrito' (pictured) is known for its plump, densely-packed foliage. The leaves regularly break off, particularly if touched, and they will often land in neighbouring pots and take root. Water moderately throughout the summer and sparingly during the winter. Plants are liable to rot off if overwatered in winter months. Grow in full sunlight for best growth, in a hanging basket.

Sedum palmeri, **Palmer's sedum,** comes from Mexico. It forms dense clumps of small rosettes on stems that are upright in the beginning but soon flop over. It's best grown in a hanging basket or somewhere it can pour over the sides. Bright yellow, star-shaped flowers appear in late winter to spring.

SEDEVERIA
Sedeveria is a hybrid between *Sedum* and *Echeveria,* the leaves are *Sedum*-like, but the shape owes something to *Echeveria*. Or you could easily confuse them with *Pachyphytum* or *Pachyveria*. *Sedeveria* 'Blue Giant' has rounded, blue-green, pebble-like leaves. *Sedeveria* 'Harry Butterfield' has grey green, distinctly pointed leaves. *Sedeveria* 'Jet Beads' has longer stems with red-green bead-like leaves. *Sedeveria 'hummelii'* has pointed tips that are blushed pink, blue-grey plump foliage and a dense rosette formation. *Sedeveria* 'Sorrento' looks most like *Echeveria* with a distinct, flattened rosette, pointed leaves in dark red, seeping into green towards the centre.

PACHYPHYTUM

Pachyphytum (pictured above) are easy to confuse with *Sedum* and *Echeveria*, and this tiny genus is closely related to them, though entirely native to Mexico. The leaves look as if someone has blown them up with a pump, which is how it got its name from the ancient Greek *pachys*, thick, and *phyton*, plant. The most common species is *Pachyphytum oviferum*. The blue-green leaves are the shape of sugared almonds and covered with a delicate white bloom. It grows on rocky cliffs and likes very free-draining soil, bright light and needs temperatures above 5°C/41°F, being happiest a few degrees warmer. Water from below if you can as water will disturb the delicate bloom and mark the leaves. Coral pink flowers appear from late winter to early spring. The leaves of *Pachyphytum bracteosum* look like very satisfying beach-worn pebbles.

PACHYVERIA

Pachyveria (pictured right) is a hybrid between *Echeveria* and *Pachyphytum*. It needs to be grown in bright, sunny conditions and should be treated the same way as *Echeveria*. It gets its leaves from *Pachyphytum* and the more pronounced rosettes from *Echeveria*. *Pachyveria compactum* has slightly angular succulent leaves that make it look like something from *Star Wars*. *Pachyveria* 'Clavifolia' has blue-grey leaves with a grey-green bloom and quite a dense rosette. *Pachyveria* 'Scheideckeri' has grey-blue leaves with slightly pointed tips and a rather loose rosette.

SPRING   SUMMER   AUTUMN   WINTER

Crassula, Crassulaceae

This is a massive genus that spans many parts of the globe. It ranges from tiny annual herbs to small shrubs. Most of the cultivated varieties originate from the Eastern Cape of South Africa. The name comes from the Latin *crassus* meaning thick or swollen and refers to the fact that the leaves of this genus are plump and succulent, reflecting that they tend to grow in hot, dry places in very free-draining, rocky soil. The foliage varies in form and texture and there are some very strange members of this family. *Crassula* are best grown in full sun, which promotes the best leaf colour. Like many of these succulent types, leaf cuttings are very easy. Remove a leaf, leave it to dry for a few days so that the wound calluses over and then gently nestle the cut end into very gritty compost, only watering when you see signs of roots. Crassulas tend to do most of their growing over the winter.

54

Crassula ovata, **Jade plant** or **Money plant** (pictured), has satisfying thick, ovate, shiny, smooth leaves that grow opposite each other. The margins are edged in red, particularly when it is grown in strong light. Too strong light and the plant goes yellow-orange. You can entirely neglect a jade plant and still it seems to linger on. You can keep in it a tiny pot and it will stay tiny, or put it in a large pot and it will grow up to 2m (6ft) tall. You decide; keep potting on if you want a tree. Tiny, starry, white or pink flowers are produced in spring. Water sparingly in summer and even less so in winter.

Crassula ovata **'Hummel's Sunset'** is pretty outrageous looking with yellow striped leaves edged with orange-red.

Crassula ovata **'Hobbit'**, **Finger jade**, has curled, rounded leaves that make them appear tubular, often with pronounced pink margins if grown in the sun. The leaves flatten a bit with age.

Crassula deceptor is native to South Africa and Namibia and has dense, grey, overlapping triangular leaves that are packed along an unbranched stem so that it looks a little like a pillar. The grey leaves are often covered with light white powder that protects the leaves from drying out and harsh sunlight, which is where you'd find this one growing. Perfect for a very bright, hot, south-facing window. The tiny pinkish flowers smell delightfully sweet.

Crassula **'Gollum'** is a hybrid with tubular leaves with the tips curled into a suction cup.

Crassula muscosa, **Rattail crassula, Lizard's tail** or **Zipper plant**, the latter is the most accurate common name as the tiny, green leaves are packed around the stem so that they resemble a zip.

Crassula schmidtii is a low cushion-forming plant with small, pointed, narrow neat leaves and starry, rose-pink flowers from autumn to spring.

SPRING   SUMMER   AUTUMN   WINTER

Kalanchoe, Crassulaceae

These come from Madagascar and include that terrible table decoration *Kalanchoe blossfeldiana* with its lurid orange flowers. Thankfully the genus is large and there are some brilliant ones well worth growing.

Kalanchoe beharensis is known as elephant's ear because its leaves are the shape and colour of those of an elephant. The leaves are covered with fine hairs; on younger leaves these are white, but with age these turn brown, giving rise to its other name, felt plant. The plant will reproduce asexually on its leaf margins, particularly if it is stressed.

Kalanchoe pumila, **Flower dust plant** (pictured), is native to Madagascar and is a dwarf plant growing to 30cm high, often grown in hanging baskets. It flowers from late winter to early spring and is often covered in violet-pink flowers. Once the flowers are over, cut off the spent heads and reduce watering until new growth resumes. The plant needs a bit of a rest after all that blooming. This plant needs bright, sunny conditions and won't be happy if the temperature drops below 12.5°C/55°F.

In winter, in order to get them back into flower, grow them on a south-facing window, reducing the watering in early autumn until flowering so that the soil just begins to dry out. In summer you can feed with a liquid feed, every two weeks; this will encourage flowering, though these are not plants shy to flowering.

56

Frithia pulchra, Baby toes, Elephant's baby toe, Aizoaceae

This is only found wild in one place in the world, growing in rocky scrubland in Gauteng province, South Africa. The leaves are modified into window-like structures that are buried so they are just visible on the surface of the rocky soil. Clusters of leaves appear out of the ground and in the right conditions bright, cactus-like, pink flowers cover the plant.

The leaves have clear windows at the apex and are club-shaped, blue-grey beneath. The window protects the cells from extremely harsh light and heat, so these are plants that can grow where little else could manage. If the drought conditions get too much the whole plant can draw itself into the ground to further protect itself. It looks very similar to the *Lithops* species, living stones, and is a pretty easy plant to keep happy; you just have to make sure it is grown in the brightest conditions you can offer and that you only water once a month maximum in the growing season and keep it dry all winter long. In short, if the club-shaped leaves are plump, leave it be.

57

Lithops, Aizoaceae

Lithops, living stones, are amazing little plants that have similar windows to *Frithia*, but because these are tasty things they need further protection from hungry desert herbivores, so they mimic stones. Each stem consists of two swollen leaves that are fused together with two smaller leaves between. At 5cm (2in) wide and 2.5cm (1in), these are not houseplants that are going to make a huge impact, but they are fascinating and very easy to grow from seed. There are numerous species to try. Sow the seed in a tray of very well-drained compost, a 70:30 grit:compost mix should work. Top off with more gravel and then wait, patiently. In two or three years you'll have your own living pebbles to admire. You don't have to water these from autumn to spring, then water sparingly throughout the summer. They must be grown in bright, sunny conditions and are ideal for hot south-facing windows. In late summer, daisy-like flowers appear, opening only when the sun is out.

Senecio, Ragworts, Asteraceae

Senecio is in the daisy family and our common European ragwort is a sibling, not that you'd necessarily recognise this when you see the huge variation in this tribe's members. It's a huge and diverse genus that spans the globe. Succulent members grow in hot, dry, desert-like conditions, tending to have blue-green, grey-green foliage to reflect the high light intensity and plump leaves to survive drought. They are easy, low-maintenance plants perfect for sunny rooms with dry heat from radiators. They will grow leggy and the more upright forms will flop given low light and too much water. In summer months, water sparingly and give them even less in the winter months.

Senecio crassissimus, **Vertical leaf senecio**, is endemic to Madagascar with thick, purple stems producing stiff flattened, long, waxy, silver-grey leaves. Each leaf is marked with vivid purple edging

Senecio radicans, **String of bananas**. If you like the string of pearls, then the string of bananas will please you just as much. Instead of pearls or beads along the stem, there are glossy blue-green, banana-shaped, up-curved leaves. It's another scrambler from South Africa and will root wherever it touches the ground. And like the string of pearls it also has epidermal windows. This time there are two translucent lines on either side of the leaf allowing more light in. In late winter or early spring, it produces off-white, cinnamon-scented flowers.

Senecio rowleyanus, **String of pearls** (pictured, behind a *Senecio* hybrid) is possibly the most satisfying of all houseplants. It looks just like a green string of pearls. The temptation to pop the perfectly spherical leaves is almost overwhelming but please don't; go find some bubble wrap instead! The plant is native to south-west Africa where it trails along the ground; wherever the stem touches the soil surface it roots (making it very easy to propagate) and eventually forms very dense mats. However, it is the perfect hanging-basket plant. The very rounded leaves are an adaptation to dry desert conditions. Their shape means the minimum surface area is exposed to dry desert air but is still suitable for storing water. The problem is that a rounded leaf, particularly one scrambling on the soil surface, reduces the amount of light the plant can take in and thus photosynthesise. To counterbalance the roundness there is a thin, narrow, crescent-shaped clear band on what is the upper surface of the leaf. This acts as an epidermal window to allow more light into the interior of the leaf, effectively increasing the surface area of the leaf. This window is similar to those in *Frithia pulchra*. Despite the fact this plant naturally grows in intensely bright conditions, as a houseplant it will survive with just a few hours of direct sunlight, but it cannot be grown in full shade, it does need bright conditions. A very rare variegated form is worth looking out for.

Senecio talinoides subsp. *cylindricus*, sometimes sold as *S. vitalis* or *S. cylindricus*, Narrow-leaf chalk-sticks, is a low growing succulent shrub that can reach up to 1.5m (5ft) tall in the wild. Each stem is crowded at the tips with long, slender, slightly curved, upward-growing, grey-green to blue-green tubular leaves. The stems are semi-prostate, meaning they stand up for a while, but eventually end up resting on their elbows. If the plant gets too leggy, which it is very prone to do, prune it hard to the base of the stem and it will sprout new leaves. The prunings can be inserted into free-draining gritty compost and will quickly root. I have far too many of these plants for that reason.

Sansevieria, Mother-in-law's tongue, Asparagaceae

Sansevieria are native to Africa, Madagascar and southern Asia and are known as mother-in law's tongues or snake plants, referring to the spiky, flattened leaves that are mottled in a pattern-like snakeskin. The genus varies from desert succulents to thin-leaved tropical plants. Most of them form dense clumps of leaves that are arranged in a rosette around the growing point. The leaves can either be hard or soft. Hard leaves come from more arid climates and soft leaves from tropical and subtropical regions.

Hard-leaved plants need very little watering and are often cylindrical or curved to reduce the surface area exposed to dry air. Soft-leaved ones need lots of watering because they are found in areas of high rainfall.

62

Sansevieria trifasciata, **Snake plant**, is the most widely grown. Growth is slow and plants last for years; this is the one plant you can leave to your children. They thrive in warm conditions in bright light, but even if abused and left in a dark corner, still it soldiers on. They do need repotting or else they will spill out of the pot or split and they don't like to sit in water (but still they'll survive). The plant fibre in the leaves is strong enough to make bowstrings, so it's one to keep going in case the apocalypse comes!

Sansevieria trifasciata **var**. *laurentii* is probably the most widely grown, with yellow leaf margins.

Sansevieria trifasciata **'Bantel's Sensation'** has very elegant silver-white variegation and long thin leaves.

Sansevieria trifasciata **'Compacta'** is a dwarf form with yellow variegation.

Sansevieria trifasciata **'Hahnii'** is a compact form with wide leaves and silver-green variegation.

Sansevieria cylindrica, **African spear plant**, is native to Angola and has striped, elongated, greenish-grey leaves that are subcylindrical, meaning they are curved inwards so that their leaves appear rounded. This is a very drought-tolerant species and only requires watering every two to three weeks in the growing season.

Sansevieria masoniana, **Whale fin**, is a giant version that will grow up to 1.5–2m (4ft 6in–6ft) tall, though it takes a long time to do so. It has wide, mottled green leaves. It comes from the Congo and is pretty rare, but well worth growing.

Cacti

Cacti are great houseplants for the obvious reason that they don't need a great deal of water. Coming from arid and semi-arid regions, they are designed to store water in those thick fleshy stems. The leaves have been modified into spines to protect such a precious resource, thus all the photosynthesising is done by the stem, which is usually a deep green. They can get away without leaves because they grow in such bright conditions where typical leaves would frazzle. Out in the desert every part of any plant that lives there is modified to deal with extreme temperature and light conditions. Even how the spines are arranged on the stem is in part to minimise water loss, casting shadows around the most vulnerable growing parts of the plant. Cactus flowers are bright but delicate, opening very early in the morning, often closing at midday (all the nectar would evaporate away in midday heat) and opening again in the evening, when the pollinators are making the most of cooler conditions to fly.

Arid and semi-arid conditions all have soils with one thing in common – they are very free-draining, being made up of sand and other fine rock particles. The root system of cacti can be quite extensive and is often shallower than you might expect. Rain is so infrequent that animals and plants are often adapted to make use of any moisture that might appear. Desert fog and dew are two sources that can account for up to half of the water available to plants and animals in such places. Shallow roots then can quickly sup up any dew caused from condensation in the desert.

It is sometimes recommended that you grow cacti and desert plants in pots with no drainage (yes I know, I do bang on about this) and mist the plants. I can only assume this is some misguided idea about dew,

fog and dry roots. Morning dew and fog are burnt off before 9am and then the plants bask in brilliant blue skies and high temperatures; this is not the same thing as deciding to mist a plant at 11am on a grey day in the city. At worst, this could cause the plant to rot and at best it is pointless. Water your cacti, and grow them in pots with drainage holes. The closest you have to desert conditions in your house is next to a sunny or bright window or skylight. There are a few forest-growing epiphytes, such as *Rhipsalis,* that make great houseplants, but don't want to be in such bright conditions and need semi-shade.

During the winter, many cacti go into a rest period and will need cooler night-time temperatures of 8–10°C/46–50°F. Central heating and radiators are not a great problem for this lot; just remember that if they are next to a heat source they will need water to prevent them from shrivelling.

Cacti need much more regular watering than you might imagine. In spring and summer they will need watering freely, allowing excess water to drain away as they should never be left to sit in water. The compost should dry out between watering; constantly moist compost will cause many cacti to rot. Forest types, such as *Rhipsalis*, prefer to be somewhere with a humid atmosphere; your bathroom can be perfect.

The one thing cacti need, and which is often forgotten, is good air circulation throughout the summer. If the weather is guaranteed to be good, give them a breather outside. It is also worth feeding cacti with specialist cacti food once a month in spring and summer. From early autumn onwards you need to encourage a period of rest, so reduce watering to allow the compost to dry out completely before watering again.

Cacti are broadly in two categories, winter-growing/ summer-dormant and summer-growing/winter-dormant. Think of them like deciduous trees – they need to stop growing for a while and have a rest period and during this time they need very little or no water. As they come out of this rest period, they need to be freely watered as they prepare for the next season of growth. Certain desert cacti need a complete period of rest from watering in winter, though if they are near a heat source you may have to adjust for this.

If your cactus is winter-flowering, such as Christmas cactus, *Schlumbergia*, then it will require warmth and watering in order to flower and its rest period will be in the summer. It is possible to damage cactus with too much kindness. Many species are opportunist when it comes to storing water; if it's available they will try and pump their cells full of the stuff. If you see the skin splitting or marking from over expanding, ease off on the amount of water. The barrel cactus, *Echinocactus*, seem particularly susceptible to this.

It is best to water cacti from below for several reasons. In a temperate climate, getting the cactus wet can cause all sorts of moulds to grow on them and potentially rot them. In bright light, wetting a cactus can cause the skin to scorch and burn – in nature you'd never get sun and rain at the same time in an arid or semi-arid habitat. Finally, many cacti take up all the pot and if you water from above the roots will receive very little. Watering from below means the roots get what they need and the top remains dry. You must always drain off any excess – cacti hate to sit in water. Tap water is not ideal for cacti and often causes an excess of nutrients and minerals to build up in the soil. Many cacti growers either use soft water, such as rainwater, brought indoors

so that it is room temperature, or modify tap water with ½ tablespoon of white wine vinegar per 9 litres (16 pints) of water. Many winter-dormant species will shrivel up a little over the winter if they are not watered because they grow in places where the night-time temperature can drop below freezing and they shrivel so that their cells don't burst if this happens. I guess it's their version of anti-freeze. If your plants shrivel and they are not near a heat source like a radiator, do not be tempted to water them. Wet soil will do them more harm than good. However, if your cactus shrivels up in the summer months (or its growing season) this is a sign that you are being a little too mean with water. The surest sign that your cactus is coming out of its dormant period is new spines at the top of the plant – when you see this happen start watering again.

SPRING   SUMMER   AUTUMN   WINTER

***Echinocereus,* Hedgehog cactus, Barrel cactus, Cactaceae** (pictured), gets its name from the Greek *echinos*, meaning hedgehog and *cereus*, meaning candle. A candle with hedgehog spines – and many of them do look just like that. The most famous species is the barrel cactus, native to the southern U.S. and Mexico, it can reach impressive widths and has a deep green barrel with terrifying yellow spines. Sadly, the barrel cactus is now threatened in its natural habitats, with only a few wild stands of specimens left.

***Echinocactus grusonii,* Golden barrel cactus, Golden ball cactus, Cactaceae**, is a spherical, globe-shaped cactus that often grows in clumps in the wild. A mature plant can reach over 1m (3ft) wide and lives for around 30 years. Mature plants have numerous pronounced ribs, not apparent in younger plants. The spines are very sharp, in various shades of yellow and sometimes slightly curved. Small, yellow flowers appear in a crown, but the plant needs to be at least 20 years old before they emerge. They need a minimum temperature of 12°C/54°F in the winter and minimal watering; excess water in the rest period will lead to rotting.

***Echinopsis,* Hedgehog cactus, Sea-urchin cactus, Cactaceae** (pictured)
Echinopsis are all native to South America, found growing in sandy or rocky soils on hillsides and between rock crevices. They have large, beautiful flowers that appear in the evening and last a couple of days during the summer. They are winter-dormant species, needing very little, if any, water. They also need a cold period at this time – the night-time temperature should be somewhere around 5-10°C/40–50°F with a day-time temperature of around 15°C/60°F. The cold rest period is paramount for flowering to occur the following summer. A bright, cool window is ideal. Even during the summer, the soil should never be saturated as the fibrous root system is very liable to rot. *Echinopsis subdenudata* is native to Bolivia and has a darkish green, ribbed body with woolly aureoles that hide very small, very sharp spines. Young plants are globular in shape, but become more columnar with age. As it doesn't have many spines it will mark easily, particularly if it's allowed to get wet and then scorch in the sun, so put it somewhere with some shade, out of direct sunlight.

Cephalocereus senilis, **Old man cactus, Cactaceae**, is native to eastern Mexico where it is considerably threatened in the wild, but widespread in cultivation. It has a very striking appearance, the columnar body covered in a shaggy coat of long, white hairs like an old man's beard. In the wild it can grow up to 15m (50ft) tall. As it ages the hairs, which are a very good form of insulation, get less prominent and start to disappear because the stem is toughening up to make it less susceptible to frost or sunburn. It's tempting to want to stroke the fluffy hairs but they belie the cactus' true nature as beneath them are vicious, yellow central spines. The brighter the position the more vigorously the hairs grow, so this cactus loves a sunny windowsill. Like most cacti, it is best watered from below as it's liable to rot if watered from above, and only water sparingly over the winter.

68

Epiphyllum, Orchid cacti, Cactaceae

Orchid cacti are another big group of epiphytic cacti native to Central America, most growing in tropical rainforests. They have large, exotic blooms that faintly resemble orchids. Many species are night flowering, blooming for just one evening, with a delicious, heady scent to attract moths.

Most plants in cultivation are hybrids with flattened, dark green stems that grow in many different directions. They are nearly always grown in hanging baskets because in pots they topple over. Bright flowers tend to appear at the end of the stems and can be yellow, pink, lavender, orange and green.

As these are jungle plants they like humid conditions and bright, but indirect light. Sunlight will scorch the stems and the plants should be watered freely in spring and summer, allowing the top centimetre (½in) of the compost to dry out between watering. In the winter you can considerably reduce watering but never let the plants completely dry out. They need a minimum winter temperature of 4–7˚C/40–45˚F.

SPRING   SUMMER   AUTUMN   WINTER

Cereus, Cactaceae

Cereus was one of the first genera of cactus to be described – a group of large columnar cacti that come from South America. They are mostly branching, tree-like cacti with angular or distinctly ribbed stems. The flowers open at night and are largely pollinated by moths. As they are night blooming the flowers tend to be pale to attract the moths in moonlight. The name *cereus* is derived from the Greek for wax.

Cereus uruguayanus is a columnar cactus with bluish-green stems that often branch once matured. The cacti are native to Brazil and Argentina where the plants can reach up to 10m (33ft) tall. As cacti go, these are fast growing and if you find yours taking over you can prune it back and several new stems will arise from the cut. As it grows fast it likes water, but hates soggy feet so give it good drainage and allow it to dry out a bit between watering, but water freely. It likes a warm position, low humidity and bright light. It's ideal for a sunny south-, east- or west-facing window and keep it away from shade.

Opuntia microdasys, Bunny ear cactus, Cactaceae

Opuntia are best known for the species *Opuntia ficus-indica*, the Indian fig or prickly pear, with bright red fruit that are edible (as are the pads that are more often cooked). They are sweet and most delicious, but don't taste much like figs. This is a large species that would be hard to grow indoors as it is very sensitive to a lack of oxygen around its roots and would resent pot life. However, *Opuntia microdasys* is much happier in a pot where it grows to a maximum 60cm (3ft) tall, quite slowly. The plant is known as bunny ear because it's usually sold when it has two secondary pads at the top of the first large pad, making it look like a cartoon bunny. This is a cruel joke of a name because there is little that makes you want to stroke this one. The pads are spineless but, instead, have glochids which are thinner than a human hair and appear in little clusters all over the pad – there are hundreds per cluster and at the slightest disturbance they drop off. Brush your hand accidently against this one and you'll have miniscule needle-like splinters that are a pain to pull out and you feel like you're undergoing some sort of electrical shock therapy as this happens. This is not a plant for children or cats which like to rub up against things, but is a plant for someone who is careful and cautious.

It needs bright light, so place it in south-, west- or east-facing windows in direct light. It needs very little, if any, water in the winter (only water it if it is near a heat source and starting to shrivel up) and room temperatures somewhere around 15–21°C/60–70°F, with slightly lower temperatures of 10–15°C/50–60°F in the winter.

Disocactus flagelliformis, Rattail cactus, Cactaceae

The rattail cactus is from Mexico and is very closely related to *Epiphyllum*. I think it might be my favourite cactus of all. This is not surprising as it's been a much-loved houseplant since it was introduced into European cultivation in the mid 1600s. Very little is known about its natural growing conditions but it can be either a lithophyte (likes growing out of rocks) or an epiphyte in very dry Mexican forests. It has long, cylindrical stems that are covered in fine hairs and bright pink flowers in spring and summer.

  Grow this one in bright conditions; it can handle a south-facing window with direct light. Water freely in spring and summer, making sure the compost is moist but not wet. Water sparingly through the winter – just enough to make sure the stems don't completely dry out. Discoloured or old stems can be removed in late winter to make room for new growth. This cactus benefits from repotting often, every 1–2 years, and although it does not need repotting into a large container it benefits from new soil as it's quite hungry. It's worth poking a chopstick into the soil every so often to aerate it as it likes oxygen-rich soils.

Rhipsalis, Cactaceae

Rhipsalis are very strange-looking cacti. They are epiphytes, meaning they grow harmlessly on other plants, and to make things even stranger, they grow in tropical rainforest. So you might not even think they are cacti when you first see them. Like many cacti, they don't have true leaves, just succulent stems that do the job of both storing water and photosynthesising. They all have long, drooping stems that can either be fairly thick and flattening, or thin and cylindrical and, if spines are present, they only appear at the juvenile stage, meaning that they are a friendly bunch.

This is a large genus found growing predominately in New World tropical rainforests where they grow high up in the branches of forest trees. There are also a few species growing in the tropical areas of Africa, making it the only cactus genus that is found in both the Old and New World (great botanist pub quiz fact). As these are forest epiphytes, they like dim, shaded conditions and high humidity, which is rare for a cactus. They're great plants for bathrooms.

Most are dainty plants to grow in hanging baskets where they hang down like a great flop of hair. At maturity then can reach 60–90cm (3–4ft) long, but in pots they generally remain smaller. Most have cylindrical stems, with pink or cream flowers followed by berries in winter.

Rhipsalis baccifera, **Mistletoe cactus** (pictured), is the cactus that crossed the ocean and can be found in tropical Central and South America and in tropical Africa and Sri Lanka. It has cylindrical stems with very fine white hairs, green-white flowers that are followed by white berries. It grows up to 90cm (3ft) long and 60cm (2ft) wide and does look remarkably like mistletoe, particularly if you imagine that you're a homesick European sailor who's been on the sea for too long. Water freely, every month, easing up a little in winter. Do not grow in direct light. Never let the compost get sodden as this will rot the plant. This cactus will tolerate drought, but the stems tend to shrivel up.

Rhipsalis pilocarpa, **White-haired mistletoe cactus**, is native to Brazil. It is covered in fine white hairs and the young growth can be particularly hairy. White hairs in cactus are usually a sign that the plant grows in a cooler or brighter environment than hairless cacti, and they are there as protection. In this case, it indicates a need for light and this one needs to be grown in bright, but not direct sunlight. Water freely year-round, easing off in winter. It will be drought tolerant for short periods of time.

Carnivorous plants

Carnivory in plants is considered in evolutionary adapativity as a last resort. Eating insects is such a resource-hungry process that things have to be pretty bad to go down this route. The reason plants decide to eat insects is because they grow in such nutrient-poor soil. There are very few examples of plants eating anything other than insects, though there is a *Puya* in Peru that eats sheep, which is the stuff of nightmares if you have a woolly coat (that's how it captures the sheep), and *Nepenthes*, tropical pitcher plants, catch small mammals and reptiles.

Carnivorous plants are almost exclusively found in wet, acidic conditions where the soil has almost no nitrogen, low phosphorous and in some cases low calcium too. What these conditions lack in basic nutrients they make up for in water and light. You never find carnivorous plants growing in deep shade (this is something to remember when placing your plant in your home) or in dry conditions. In cost–benefit terms, if a plant doesn't have to fight for light and water it is worth taking some of that energy necessary to make useful photosynthetic leaves and turn them into traps. The intricate, complex traps of carnivorous plants are just modified leaves.

There are several types of traps: pitfalls (*Nepenthes* and *Sarracenia*), sticky traps (*Drosera* and *Pinguicula*), snap traps (Venus flytraps), bladdertraps (bladderworts) and lobster pots (*Sarracenia* and *Nepenthes*).

The most common houseplant is the Venus flytrap which has two modified leaves hinged along the centre, and in the middle of each leaf are three trigger hairs. These are sensitive to touch and when two or more are bent, a complex chemical chain of acids is stimulated causing the leaves to snap shut. The insect is then locked into a cage where it slowly dies; the more it struggles the tighter the leaves close in until hermetically shut, when the leaves turn into a stomach, secreting digestive enzymes until the insect is absorbed over a two-week period. Once this occurs, the leaves reopen for another one or two meals before becoming unresponsive. If you cruelly keep triggering the traps they give up and die, which is what many a small child has done to these poor plants. Venus flytraps need live insects because that process of tightening around the insect for digestion can't occur unless there's a struggle. Venus flytraps do eat flies, but they are quite hard to catch and the majority of their food is ants, beetles, spiders and grasshoppers. Most houses don't have that many insects in them and if they are not over- triggered by small children, most venus flytraps die from hunger.

Why would insects willingly walk into the leaves? Well, there's a deceptive trick (requiring even more plant resources; back to the cost–benefit analysis of leaf modification): Venus flytrap leaves look, to a fly at least, like a bit of rotting meat. They have mottled pink colouration along the middle of the leaves, and on top of this they lure many of their prey in with nectar that is secreted along the teeth at the edge of the trap.

Stickytraps are just like flypaper, or better than flypaper because many of them move. The leaves of sticky traps are studded with sticky, mucilage-secreting glands that trap tiny flies, gnats and wandering insects on their surface and then slowly suck them dry. In the case of *Drosera*, sundews, they are mobile, wrapping around their prey as they stick to them. These plants are so good at trapping insects that they have given up producing enzymes to assimilate soil-born nitrates and instead get all their nitrogen from their prey.

Pitfall traps are most commonly found in pitcher plants, such as *Sarracenia* and *Nepenthes*, but also in some bromeliads. In this carnivorous group the leaf is modified so that it possesses an internal chamber that fills with water and digestive enzymes, creating a nitrogen soup that is eventually reabsorbed by the plant. Some pitfall traps are passive; prey are attracted by nectar bribes and the lip of the trap is waxy and slippery so insects fall into the trap. Other traps have more active, precarious lips where the insects are lured into thinking they are going to find an endless supply of nectar or rotting meat to lay their eggs in, and then the lip is so slippery and hazardous they fall

in. In some cases, there's a lid at the top of the trap (as in *Sarracenias*), which has two benefits – it keeps rain from diluting the enzyme soup in the trap and small insects are forced to endlessly climb it in a bid to get out and inevitably many tire and fall in.

Lobster pots are similar to pitfall traps in having a chamber where the insect is digested, but they differ in that the chamber is easy to climb into but impossible to climb out of because of inward-pointing bristles that force the prey to move in only one direction.

Drosera, Sundews, Droseraceae

Sundews use a sticky-trap system of fine, usually red, hairs, each with a mucilaginous sticky globe at the end. They have tiny, very pretty flowers. They must never be allowed to dry out and should be grown in an ericaceous compost mixed 3 parts compost : 1 part sharp sand. However, you'll rarely need to repot them. In summer months, you can keep pots permanently standing in a centimetre (½in) of water to achieve the right moisture and humidity.

Drosera capensis comes from South Africa. It forms rosettes of long, strap-like leaves with showy red tentacles and rose-pink flowers; mature plants trail with numerous rosettes in a single pot. It likes bright, sunny conditions, it must be watered with rainwater and can withstand temperatures as low as 3°C /37°F.

Drosera filiformis, **Threadleaved sundew**, is a northern hemisphere form from America and has a resting bud stage, known as a hibernaculum, meaning that in winter it dies right back to a cluster of buds. Although this hibernaculum won't grow during winter, it must not dry out. This plant has thin leaves, up to 20cm (8in) long, that unfurl in the most beautiful way in spring. In summer, it has large, rose-pink flowers.

Drosera rotundifolia, **Roundleaved sundew**, is another one with the resting bud stage in winter. It has circumboreal distribution – through the forested area of the northern hemisphere including northern Europe, Siberia, Korea, Japan and North America. It has a rosette of long, thin leaves and the end of each leaf is spoon-shaped and covered in bright red glands. In summer, it has white or pink flowers.

76

Dionaea muscipula, Venus flytrap, Droseraceae

The Venus flytrap is native to the subtropical wetlands of the East Coast of America, which are sadly under a lot of pressure. The loss of suitable habitat means that these beguiling plants are considered vulnerable in their native range. The traps can be green with a red tinge or completely red, and secrete nectar along the base of their teeth to lure prey in. The teeth on the edge of the traps are actually fairly wide, which means that smaller insects can wander out. Because the cost–benefit of digesting a small insect is too low, it's only worth trapping larger prey.

Venus flytraps are notoriously difficult to grow. Although they are less humidity-dependent than other carnivorous plants, they do need moist conditions and don't like being cramped in a pot. You need to repot every year if your specimen is doing well. They need a winter's rest, but during the summer they can sit permanently in a saucer of water. Soft or rainwater is essential and they must be watered from below. They require full sun for a large part of the day to thrive, which is hard to achieve on a windowsill. They must never be allowed to dry out. I have had success growing them in a terrarium, where they remain moist, on a sunny windowsill, but it's very important that the terrarium opening is big enough to allow insects in.

Propagate by division or seed sowing.

77

Pinguicula, Butterworts, Lentibulariaceae

Butterworts are perhaps the easiest carnivorous plants to grow. They are globally distributed, found in Europe, North America, South America and Asia, with both tropical and temperate species. For houseplants, tropical species are the easier to grow. *Pinguicula*, comes from the Latin *pinguis*, meaning fat, and butterworts have neat rosettes of rounded, golden-green leaves that are covered with tiny glands of sticky, enzyme-digesting mucilage that make the leaves look covered in fat. The golden colouring of the leaves gives the impression they might have been sculpted out of butter. This would be reason enough to grow them, but on top of this they have delightful violet-like flowers in hues of purple.

Out of all houseplants, *Pinguicula* are genuinely good flytraps, particularly if you get compost gnats, as these are their favourite prey. The little gnats are attracted to the buttery deliciousness of the leaves and get stuck so the beautiful leaves are soon covered in little black dots. Not exactly pretty, but when you remember the plant is doing you a favour by feeding itself all is forgiven. The more insects they trap, the more flowers you get. By winter, however, and in their native habitat, the insect haul tends to dry up and as the conditions get colder the plants often rest. In temperate species, this takes the form of a resting bud phase and all the leaves die back. In Mexican and other tropical species, the large, sticky leaves die off but are replaced by a smaller, tighter rosette of leaves that aren't sticky as there are no insects to catch.

Pinguicula moranensis var. *caudata*, **Mexican butterwort** (pictured), has a rosette of roundish, golden-yellow to olive-green leaves with wonderful colour variations if grown in full sun, especially towards the autumn when they turn varied attractive reds. In winter leaves die off to be replaced by smaller, non-sticky leaves. In summer, beautiful salmon-pink to rose-pink flowers appear and sometimes again in midwinter. In their native habitat, these butterworts grow in mountain forests that are deep in mist for most of the year, making this a good subject for bathrooms. If you don't want red leaves, don't grow in direct sunlight. You can grow this species outdoors in the summer, but it will need to come into the warm in winter as they shouldn't go below 7°C/45°F.

SPRING   SUMMER   AUTUMN   WINTER

Sarracenia, North American pitcher plant, Sarraceniaceae

Sarracenia probably have the strangest and most beguiling of all carnivorous flowers. They are like strange props from a 1950s World Fair and come in creams, yellows and crimson. Growing as big stands of plants in their native habitats, they look quite stunning. They'll look equally fabulous in your house and can happily spend the summer outside if you have the space. Many can spend the winter outside too, surviving down to minus conditions. But in my experience, hot summer temperatures are the way to keep them happy and we don't often grow them outdoors, which is why I'm including them as indoor plants.

The leaves of pitcher plants are equally as good looking as the flowers and so good at eating insects that you can often hear a sort of strange buzzing as numerous flies flail around in the digestive soup. The pitchers can smell a bit, not a strong whiff but not one that you'd want on your dining-room table. Pitfall traps release a strong, intoxicating nectar that gets the flies a little tipsy and down they tumble, then aren't able to crawl back up the shiny surface of the inner trap. The pitchers die off toward the end of autumn, and, although they don't exactly look pretty as they do this, the plant is absorbing all the nutrient goodness so trimming them off would defeat the process. By winter they will have gone paper dry and brown and, as long as there's no water left inside them, you can then happily trim them back. In summer, they will need to sit in a couple of centimetres (1in) of water but no more. In winter, they can rest, but they shouldn't be allowed to completely dry out.

There is a correlation between pitcher colour and flowers – if the pitchers are red, the flower will be too, and so on. *Sarracenia* will withstand a little shade but do best in bright conditions and will thrive in direct sunlight, as long as they don't dry out. They will not tolerate artificial light. If specimens are doing well they are easy to divide in spring.

Sarracenia flava var. flava, Yellow pitcher plant (pictured), has greenish-yellow pitchers and matching coloured flowers. It's native from Florida to Alabama, growing in pine barrens and bogs.

Sarracenia leucophylla has tall, red-veined pitchers and ruby-red flowers. Native to Florida, it grows in bogs and pine barrens (which are wetter than the name suggests).

A happy plant can grow huge, with a pitcher up to 1.2m (4ft) tall, so this is an ambitious one for many houses, but if you have the space, go for it.

Sarracenia purpurea subsp. purpurea is a smaller plant, growing to 30cm (12in) high with short, red to purple pitchers and deep red-purple flowers.

Nepenthes, Tropical pitcher plants or Monkey cups, Nepenthaceae

These tropical pitcher plants are native to the Far East, particularly Borneo, and they make their North American counterparts look relatively sane in design. These are scrambling climbers and lianas; their roots are in the cool and wet of the forest floor, but their leaves scramble up trees. There are two distinct groups: upland and lowland types. The lowland sorts are used to growing in hot, humid conditions, whereas the upland ones grow in tropical mountain forests and these are the ones that are more common as houseplants.

High in their tropical mountain homes they enjoy warm to cool but humid days, and cool, humid nights. They will not be happy in conditions below 8°C/46°F. As these plants are from areas of high humidity they will need misting if they are grown in dry rooms.

My happiest *Nepenthes* is growing near the kitchen sink. A bright bathroom would be an equally good space, but above a radiator is not. Very bright conditions will turn the leaves red and direct sunlight will scorch and damage the leaves. Remember these naturally climb up the trunks of other tropical trees and thrive in shaded conditions. Although the root should be kept damp, they should not be waterlogged. My plant has gone through periods of drought and survived, but hardly thrived. If curious, cut open your pitcher to see what it has been digesting (pictured below). *Nepenthes* are one of the few carnivorous plants that thrive from being fed in the summer months. Use an orchid feed or a tomato feed every other week as these plants like high levels of nitrogen. Happy plants will start to lengthen as they seek something to climb up and, if this is undesirable, then you can cut back ungainly plants in spring, cutting back by a third to a suitable leaf.

Lowland *Nepenthes* are the easiest to grow in most homes but they want the night-time temperature to remain above 16°C/60°F in the winter and around 20°C/68°F in the summer.

Nepenthes rafflesiana and its hybrids are the easiest lowland types. It has pale green pitchers with red spots. It can withstand temperatures down to 13°C/55°F but is happier at 16°C/60°F and can grow up to 1.5m (4ft 6in) high. It is best grown in a hanging basket.

Highland *Nepenthes* thrive in cool winter conditions and do best in well-ventilated areas. I tend to stick my plants outside in the summer, hanging the basket off the washing line where I can daily drench it in water if the temperature rises above 21°C/70°F. In winter, they prefer temperatures around 8–13°C/46–55°F.

Bromeliads, Bromeliaceae

Bromeliads are mostly epiphytic plants, usually found growing on trunks and branches of trees and shrubs. They get no nourishment from their hosts; they are merely there to anchor themselves aloft in a good position for light and water. Some are lithophytic, meaning that they grow on rocks, and a few live in the margins between forest and beach which is where the most famous bromeliad, the pineapple, comes from.

Many tropical bromeliads form a very distinct rosette of leaves that looks like an urn. The top of the leaves are shaped so as to funnel water into the reservoir below. Falling leaves and animal debris collect in these reservoirs breaking down to make a liquid feed which is absorbed by special glands at the base of the leaf. These unique ponds are important habitats in the tropical rainforest – tree frogs almost exclusively lay their eggs in them and the reservoirs act as a crèche for the tadpoles.

Once mature, most bromeliads bloom and then die, though nearly all reproduce themselves with numerous offsets, known as pups. These pups nourish themselves from the dying parent and once they are a good size – at least a quarter of the size of the parent – they can be cut off and grown separately.

Despite being epiphytic, many bromeliads are sold in pots, which is fine as long as the compost is free-draining and open. Ordinary potting compost mixed with orchid-grade bark is ideal. Water the roots sparingly in a pot, but mist the leaves often, particularly if they're in a room with the central heating on high. Remember, these plants are from the rainforest, so they thrive in high humidity. They'll love a sunny bathroom, or a bright windowsill near the kettle, but in a dark, hot, dry room they will wither and die.

The flowers tend to be small and delicate, but they are borne on brilliantly coloured bracts that persist long after the blooms fade. These bracts can be electric blue, bright neon pink or orange. Once the bract dies, so, eventually, does the mother plant. However, you should have numerous offsets surrounding the mother. Once the pups are a quarter of the size of the mother plant, cut her off and leave the new plants room to expand.

Tillandsia, Air plants, Bromeliaceae

This is the largest and most widely spread group of all bromeliads. They are found in all sorts of habitats: forests, mountains, Central and South American deserts, southern United States and the West Indies. They can be found in environments from tropical rainforests to the extremely dry and cold elevations of the Andes, to the Louisiana swamps or draping themselves over cacti in Mexico. In Peru, they are found growing in deserts where the only moisture is seasonal fog. Most bromeliads on the market are hybrids created by Dutch breeders.

They are known as air plants because they are epiphytic – living harmlessly on other plants, usually nestled into tree limbs or hanging off them. Most are true epiphytes, meaning that they need to be grown fixed to something such as bark, cork or branches. But some of them take epiphyte to a new level and are known as aerophytes, meaning that they have no roots and grow on shifting desert soils. In general, the thinner the leaves the more likely they are to grow in rainy areas, and the thicker the leaves the more likely they are to come from areas subject to drought. Most species absorb water and nutrients through their leaves from rain, dew and, in the case of the extreme desert types, dust. Those attached to trees or rocks will absorb nutrients from decaying leaf and insect matter. They do this through specialised hairs known as trichomes – very fine epidermal outgrowths that trap moisture, dew and even fog to help the plant survive.

In recent years, they have become incredibly popular houseplants, nearly always sold unattached to anything, like aerophytes, even though most of them aren't this specific group. Instead, they tend to be offsets or pups that have yet to grow the roots they need to anchor them. Whether you attach them to something or not is neither here nor there, though if not attached they may need watering a little more often. Usually they will need misting 1–3 times a week. If they dry out, then dunking them in water is a quick method of rehydration and, as good practice, do this once a month, making sure they are allowed to dry out quickly. As their name suggests, they like to grow where there is good air circulation. Leaving them to sit in any sort of moisture will just cause them to go mouldy and rot. Cork, bark or actual tree branches (driftwood works well) make good homes for them, hung vertically so that water drains off.

Tillandsia brachycaulos is native to Central America and is found growing in sub-mesic areas, meaning it likes moisture. When it's about to flower the whole plant blushes red. This species tolerates a wild range of conditions. Its soft green leaves would normally suggest a preference for shade, but it can handle direct morning sun if you drench it with water every other day.

Tillandsia cyanea, **Pink quill**, is from the forests of Ecuador. It has thin, re-curved leaves that form a stemless rosette, the flower is a paddle-shaped, almost flattened spike that is bright pink with delicate violet-purple flowers in spring and autumn.

Tillandsia ionantha, **Blushing bride**, is a popular species because it's hardy and low-maintenance. When not in flower, the whole plant is grey-green, but as it flowers the inner leaves blush red, contrasting with the violet flower spikes. It grows on tree trunks in tropical dry forests and scrub in Mexico and Central America.

Tillandsia xerographica (pictured previous page) is the biggest air plant that you're likely to find. It grows naturally in very dry and thorny scrub in southern Mexico, Guatemala and El Salvador where the temperature is 22–28°C/72–82°F. In order to receive the most light, this plant likes to grow on the highest branches. In your house it needs heat and light and wants occasional misting. Also submerge it in water at least once a month for around 15 minutes (or take it into a lukewarm shower!) Once you have drenched it you must turn it upside down because, if water collects in the broadest part of the base of the leaves, it will rot very quickly.

SPRING   SUMMER   AUTUMN   WINTER

Aechmea fasciata, **Urn plant** (pictured right) comes from rainforests in Brazil. It grows to 50cm (20in) tall and has grey-green leaves banded with silvery white. When it's about to flower, a bright pink bract appears that is covered in fragile blue flowers. Make sure that an urn plant never dries out. Aechmas need bright conditions and will not tolerate too much shade.

SPRING   SUMMER   AUTUMN   WINTER

Ananas comosus* var. *variegatus (pictured left) is the prettiest pineapple. Pineapples are terrestrial rather than epiphytic and grow on the edge of the rainforest where it meets the beach. They like very free-draining conditions and need high humidity to fruit. They prefer temperatures around 21-27°C/70-80°F. Rather than buying a plant, you can use a shop-bought pineapple. Choose a specimen with a healthy top and cut off the top, removing the bottom layer of leaves to reveal the thick stem. Trim off any 'fruit' as this will rot and pot up the top in compost mixed with horticultural sand (builders' sand has too much lime in it). Water sparingly to begin with until you see roots or new growth, then water well. It needs to be grown in good light.

Guzmania (pictured above) is an epiphytic genus from Brazil with many species and hybrids for sale. The flowering bracts last many months. *Guzmania lingulata* var. *minor* is a compact variety with a red bract and glossy green foliage. It needs a minimum night time winter temperature of 10°C/50°F and bright but not direct light.

Neoregalia (pictured above) are mostly from Brazil and are epiphytic, known for their wonderfully coloured, tooth-edged foliage that usually turns bright red or pink as the plant is about to flower. This is to tell the pollinator to return soon for a treat. The bract is produced in the middle of the central urn and more often than not this mother urn dies off after flowering. *Neoregalia carolinae* forma *tricolor*, Blushing bromeliad, turns bright pinkish red in the middle of its green and yellow striped leaves as it is about to flower. It needs bright, but not direct light conditions.

Yucca, Asparagaceae

There are about 50 species of yucca, all found in the Americas, from southern Alberta in Canada down to Mexico, South America and into the Caribbean. They are found in hot and arid places, growing in rocky deserts, badlands, mountainous regions and occasionally in forests. One of the most famous species is the Joshua Tree of Joshua Tree National Park, California.

They are known for their drought tolerance. Many parts of the plant are edible or useful – the roots can be made into soap, the tough fibres in the leaves used for material and the flowers are prized in cooking, with a flavour somewhere between artichokes and asparagus.

Young plants make excellent houseplants because they are tough, drought tolerant and don't mind direct sunlight. From spring to autumn they should be watered freely, making sure the compost is moist, but never waterlogged. If you feed them as well, you'll find you get considerable growth. Over the winter, the compost should be allowed to dry out between watering. Yucca resent sitting in waterlogged soil and should never be left in a saucer full of water. If your plant outgrows its space, you can cut the stem at a desired spot and it will re-sprout in a couple of weeks. It's best to do this in spring.

Yucca gigantea, syn. *Yucca elephantipes,*
Spineless yucca (pictured) is the national flower of El Salvador and the flowers are hugely prized edibles, often eaten with eggs. Plants mature into considerable trees up to 9m (30ft) tall and 4m (13ft) wide.

Beaucarnea recurvata,
Ponytail palm, Asparagaceae

94

The ponytail palm gets its name because its leaves sprout like a ponytail on top of a bulbous trunk that looks a little like an elephant's foot. It's not actually a palm at all. The plants are native to eastern Mexico where they can grow to a ripe old age of several hundred years. The bulbous base to the trunk is known as an expanded caudex and is for the purpose of storing water during periods of drought. So this is one that you will not have to water often. Overwatering will upset it terribly, as will claggy compost – it's a good idea to poke holes with a chopstick down into the soil around the base regularly to make sure the conditions remain free draining. It prefers bright conditions and will tolerate direct light.

Grown outside with a good root system it can withstand temperatures down to -5°C/23°F, but it doesn't like a wet winter, so it's mainly grown as an indoor plant in colder climates. It is very slow growing and rarely needs repotting. If you do need to repot, do so carefully as it doesn't like its roots being damaged.

To maintain its original shape don't be tempted to snip off the ends of the leaves – they don't grow back. If a leaf tip is dead or damaged you have to wait patiently for the whole leaf to die back and then remove it. The snipped bit might look clean, but it too will start to die back and it always looks so much worse than the leaf naturally dying back.

Euphorbia

Euphorbia are a wild bunch. It's a huge family that spans the globe and comes in every shape and size conceivable, and is commonly known as spurge. As houseplants, euphorbias are masquerading as cactus, though they tend to be a bit deeper green in colour and slightly more shiny. They don't have spines. Instead they sometimes have thorns. Spines are modified leaves, thorns are modified stems. Thorns are nasty, but spines are nastier.

All euphorbias have bitter, sticky, white milky fluid with latex in it. This sap is toxic; every herbivore knows this because a tiny nick in the skin and *Euphorbia* bleed everywhere, letting everyone know how nasty their sap is. *Euphorbia* can bleed like this because the sap is pressurised. Shortly after being exposed to air it congeals. If you get the white, milky sap on you by accident, wash it off quickly. It's a horrible irritant that can cause considerable inflammation, particularly if it gets into your mouth, eyes or nose. If this happens, seek medical advice immediately. For this reason, keep euphorbias away from children and curious pets. As the sap is sticky, once it dries its very hard to wash off with just water alone. Milk is the simplest way to get it off.

Euphorbia grown as houseplants tend to be the sort found in xerophytic conditions – deserts, arid places – and thus they should be treated as succulents. The ones that look just like cacti tend to be from Madagscar and southern Africa. They need to be grown in bright conditions and are happy on south-facing windowsills, though very direct midday sun can scorch some types. They need to be watered regularly throughout the growing season, but should always be allowed to dry out between watering and should never sit in water.

***Euphorbia ingens*, Cactus spurge, Cactus euphorbia,** is a very common houseplant, native to the Americas, ranging from Patagonia to southern Canada. It is typically found growing in dry, arid, rocky conditions. With age, it produces impressive candelabra branches. To most, it looks just like a bright green cactus with thorns. It has bright red flowers that appear near the thorns. It can grow up to 12m (40ft) in the wild, though in your house it could at a push get to 2m (6½ft) tall if you offer it enough light. It needs to be grown in direct sunlight, so near a south- or west-facing window or a bright skylight. Never stand it in water for any period of time and always let it dry out completely before watering. In the winter water very sparingly, just making sure the soil doesn't become bone dry – perhaps once a month.

***Euphorbia lactea* 'Cristata', Candelabra plant, Coral plant** (pictured) is actually two plants sliced together and grafted to create a franken-plant. The bottom part is usually *Euphorbia neriifolia* and is cylindrical and deep green and the top part is *Euphorbia lactea*, which resembles coral or a brain, depending on how you see the world. It is a rare mutation that cause *Euphorbia lactea* to form a crest and can only be propagated by grafting.

It prefers full sun to partial shade. It can scorch in very bright direct light; if this happens move it slightly further away from the window. Do not overwater this plant; allow it to completely dry out between waterings as overwatering is the quickest way to kill it. Sometimes the bottom graft likes life too much and sends up a huge sucker. I like this weird combination but if you don't, chop it off (just don't get the sap on you).

Ceropegia linearis subsp *woodii*, Chain of hearts, Apocynaceae

Ceropegia is a flowering plant native to South Africa, Swaziland and Zimbabwe and was discovered by the curator of Durban Botanic Gardens in 1881, hanging from a rock in Groenberg. He later sent the plant to Kew where it flowered and everyone decided it was the perfect hanging-basket plant. This is a much-loved houseplant because it can withstand an epic amount of abuse in the form of drought. It can do this because it develops tubers with age that store water and help it through periods of drought. It also produces small round, sometimes woody-appearing, tubers along the stem. These, if cut off and stuck in new soil, will root. For this reason, the vine is known as the rosary vine.

Ceropegia naturally grows in full sun where the heart-shaped leaves develop a deep green colour. Most house conditions don't offer it quite enough light and the leaves turn pale green in such conditions. It doesn't seem to mind though. There are several forms with variegated leaves and silver foliage.

If it is happier it will flower – these are tiny, off-white little pipes with magenta-brown petals – strange, curious things that are pollinated by flies.

You can get away with watering once a month, if it's not in direct light, but in full sun, it will need to be watered regularly through the growing season, though never left to sit in water and should always be allowed to dry out between waterings. During winter, watering needs to be reduced greatly, only watering when the plump leaves start to look a little flaccid. It is often sold in tiny pots – repot the minute you get home. The more root run you give this one, the less watering you have to do.

Hoya, Asclepiadaceae

Hoyas are in the milkweed family, a fairly large genus of 200–300 tropical vines and creepers, known as waxplants, waxvines or waxflowers, referring to both the waxy-looking flowers and leaves. The name does the flowers a disservice; they are much more than that. They have five triangular, thick, waxy petals shaped like stars, borne in clusters of persistent peduncles, which are known as spurs. As these spurs are perennial and get bigger each year it's important that you don't snip them off (I don't know why you would, but just in case you're into tidying up plants, don't). To me they look like the little sugar flowers my mother used to decorate cakes with, as if they've been pressed out of sugar and delicately painted. In fact, they are made out of sugar or at least rich in nectar, and in the mornings you will often find a little drop of nectar at the end of each flower. Taste it, it's deliciously sweet.

Hoyas, like so many other houseplants, often grow epiphytically on trees, sometimes on rocks and often scrambling along the ground. If you look closely at the stems you'll see lots of little bumps; these are the beginnings of adventitious roots. If these adventitious roots touch something damp, such as soil or wet bark, they will start to grow. For this reason, it's very easy to propagate new hoyas – just find a bumpy bit of stem and peg it down into some soil. In a few weeks, you'll be able to see roots and then you can sever it from the mother plant.

Hoyas can grow in deep shade, but if you want them to flower, they need to be able to climb up to bright conditions. They are very drought resistant and can take a cycle of completely drying out through neglect and then being rescued, but again they won't flower and growing these is all about the spectacular flowers. Hoyas do best in an open soil medium that allows air to the roots so try adding bark mulch or perlite to your houseplant compost to open the mix. You often hear that hoyas like to be potbound to help them to flower but I don't think this is the case; these are plants that will withstand abuse, but as in all things in life, be kind.

Hoya carnosa is native to eastern Asia and Australia. The flowers are sweetly scented, generally light pink, but they can vary from light to dark magenta. This plant has been in cultivation for more than 200 years and there are hundreds of cultivars varying in form and foliage. Some have very dark flowers that are beautiful but hard to spot among the foliage.

Hoya carnosa 'Variegata' has pink-suffused cream margins to the dark green leaves.

Palms

Palms are in the Arecaceae family and are one of the most commonly grown plants in the world for food, fibre and shelter. They are found growing in tropical and subtropical areas and are distinguished by their large, evergreen leaves, known as fronds, arranged at the top of unbranched stems. The leaves are either fan shaped or feathered. They grow in habitats as diverse as tropical rainforests and deserts. Palms need to be kept relatively moist, during spring and summer, or when the temperatures warm up. Water them regularly, as soon as the soil feels a little dry below the surface. Palms like good drainage and won't be happy in a pot that doesn't drain well. The quickest way to kill a palm is to let it sit in water. They benefit from the whole plant having a wash once in a while (a shower works well). Most palms like good light conditions, but will scorch in direct midday light. Palms often have shallow root systems and don't like to be disturbed, so only pot them when they are completely potbound. Feed palms once a month during the growing season and they'll grow quite rapidly. Yellow or brownish fronds can be a sign of potassium deficiency, which is common in palms. Finally, palm fronds take a long time to die back and it's easy to want to trim and tidy the plant up, but they draw nutrients from the old fronds long after they've started to yellow. Never cut your palm down to one or two new fronds and only remove the leaves when they are fully brown and papery.

104

Howea forsteriana, Kentia palm, Arecaceae

The Kentia palm is perhaps the most well known of all palms and makes a very good houseplant because it's tolerant of lower light levels than most palms, and copes with some degree of neglect. In the Victorian era it was known as the parlour palm, because most sitting rooms had one. Victorian parlours were notoriously dark and gloomy as well as polluted owing to coal fires, and the fact that the Kentia palm survived here says a lot about its tolerance to less than desirable conditions.

Kentia is the capital of the Lord Howe Island in the Tasman Sea, hence the common and Latin name. For feminists out there, *forsteriana* refers to Senator William Forster of New South Wales who was instrumental in obtaining suffrage for the women of Australia. Sadly, in its native habitat the Kentia palm is considered critically endangered, partly because it was over-collected for parlours and their like, with many plants dug up from the wild. Now there's a very strict limit on what can be collected and a limited amount of seed is taken from the wild each year. It is highly likely that your palm grew from seed collected from the island as it's an important industry there.

In the wild, these palms grow in great stands in the forest, reaching up to 18m (60ft) tall and they are incredibly elegant with their graceful, arching fronds of pinnate (feather-like) leaves. Their forest homes are subtropical and some are quite cool so, surprisingly, *Howea* can take a degree of frost for a couple of nights, but they prefer a night-time temperature of no lower than 10°C/50°F.

As a houseplant, *Howea forsteriana* is very slow growing. A plant may live in the same pot its entire life and restricting the pot size is one way to keep the palm at your desired height. They certainly only need to be repotted every 5–10 years and the roots are very fragile and resent repotting, so be very gentle.

Kentia palms can grow in low, indirect light in a north–facing room, but do better with a little more light. They can be grown in full sun but you will have to water them far more regularly. It prefers indirect light conditions and may scorch in direct sunlight. In general you can let the top layer of *Howea* soil dry out between waterings, but don't extend this dry period for more than a few days.

If it goes through a real period of drought it is very hard to resurrect a palm. If the tips start to turn yellow and then go brown this is a sign that you need to water more regularly. Another sign that the plant needs more water is if the fronds start to droop. You can ease off watering in winter, when light levels drop off, but again, don't let the plant completely dry out for an extended period of time.

It's a good idea to mist your Kentia palm or give it a warmish shower from time to time as they do tend to collect dust. Regularly misting will also prevent red spider mite that are rather keen on them. Kentia palms are poisonous to pets, so if your dog likes to chew, avoid this one.

106

Dypsis lutescens, **Golden cane palm, butterfly palm, Arecaceae** (pictured left)
The golden cane palm comes from Madagascar where it grows predominately in thickets along streams. Lovely palm fronds have distinct yellow midribs that arch outwards like butterfly wings, hence the common names. Despite being a waterside plant, it is surprisingly drought tolerant. It needs more light than the Kentia palm, preferring a bright position with indirect light. If grown in direct light you will need to water often as in good conditions a 2m (6ft) golden cane palm will transpire a litre (1¾pints) of water a day, effectively making it a living humidifier. If you find that your home feels a little parched, perhaps invest in this one and water it well.

Rhapis excelsa, **Lady palm, Arecaceae**
(pictured on page 103)
The lady palm is a broad-leaf fan palm, meaning it has palmate leaves that fan into broad, rib segments. It grows very slowly to 4m (12ft), but most mature house specimens get to around 2m (6ft) tall. It is thought to come from south China, though there are no known wild species left and it exists only in cultivation.

It makes a wonderful palm for cooler houses, as it's happy enough with temperatures above 5°C/41°F. It is also known for tolerance to low light levels and dry atmospheric conditions, plus it is fairly drought tolerant, coping with dry periods for a short while. It will need watering regularly but the top surface of the soil should be allowed to dry out between watering. In winter, watering can be considerably reduced as it very much dislikes waterlogged conditions and overwatering is the quickest way to kill it.

Cycas revoluta, Cycad, sago palm, Japanese sago
palm, Cycadaceae (pictured right)
Cycads or sago palms are native to Japan and are used
to make sago, a kind of starch. Extracting the sago
involves washing the starchy middle of the trunk and
processing the material. Goodness only knows how
someone first stumbled across this. However, cycads
are extremely poisonous to humans and pets, who
unfortunately seem to find them very palatable. Within
12 hours liver failure and all sorts of other horrors occur.

As a houseplant, as long as your pets don't nibble it,
it's an easy-going guest. Drought and cold tolerant, it
doesn't like extended frost but can survive and anything
above 5°C/41°F is fine. It is extremely slow growing,
but in the wild it can reach a considerable size with a
trunk up to 6m (20ft) round, though it will take around
a century to get there. It grows best in bright conditions
with indirect light. Bright sunlight may cause scorching.

It's a beautiful houseplant with a wonderful symmetry
to the dark, glossy green leaves that are arranged in a
feathered rosette from the shaggy trunk. The leaflets
are needle-like and glossy. Both male and female plants
are needed for seed to be produced; the male cones
are yellow and very striking. It is not a true palm, but a
gymnosperm. These are an ancient group of plants that
were around at the time of the dinosaurs, 65.5 million
years ago, although the species alive today are merely
12 million years old.

107

Ficus, Fig, Moraceae

Figs are a large and diverse bunch – there are tropical woody climbers, shrubs and trees. Many of the tropical species start life as an epiphyte; some remain like this, others strangle their host and some go on to bigger and better things. Nearly all the figs that we grow as houseplants come from the tropics and they like the humid, warm, wet conditions that are associated with rainforests.

Some figs have huge leaves and others tiny ones. All have one distinguishing factor – when you pull off a leaf the fig bleeds a milky white, latex sap. Often this sap is sticky and some people are sensitive to it, so I don't suggest wiping it everywhere.

Despite figs being very popular houseplants, they aren't the easiest customers. All figs are sensitive to over- and underwatering, which will cause the leaves to yellow and eventually drop. The best way to keep a fig happy is to allow the pot to dry out almost completely and then water well, so that the pot is saturated. On top of being a little fussy about water, draughts and low temperatures cause similar symptoms – one day your fig may be in full leaf and the next day naked, with all its leaves around its feet. These are temperamental sorts – just a blast of cold air from a door opening in winter can cause them to drop all their leaves.

Many figs do best when slightly potbound, so they can be considered slightly perverse as well as temperamental. With this in mind, only repot them every 2–3 years into light, fast-draining compost, adding perlite to any houseplant-potting compost. Big specimens, in the years between repotting, will benefit from top dressing in spring with fresh compost and feeding monthly with a liquid food.

If you need to prune because the plants become leggy, then try and do this in late winter so the pruning cuts will be hidden with the new flush of spring growth. All that white, latex sap blackens eventually when exposed to oxygen and any pruning cut may look rather scarred.

Figs really like being in a gang as this helps maintain atmospheric humidity, so gather up your houseplants and give your fig some friends. Try and choose friends that like to be misted because in hot, dry weather figs love a cooling down. All figs like bright conditions, but not direct sunlight and midday sunlight will scorch the leaves. Mealybug and soft scale are their main enemies on the pest front.

***Ficus benjamina,* Benjamin tree, Weeping fig**, may reach 2m (6ft) as a houseplant, but in the tropics it will grow up to 30m (100ft) high as a graceful weeping tree. It starts life as an epiphyte, but eventually becomes independent, with the oldest trees ending up with a thicket of aerial roots to support the increasingly spreading and dropping branches. It can be found growing throughout south and southeast Asia. The leaves have a pronounced drip tip,

reminding you exactly how humid they like things. Older leggy plants can be coaxed into creating aerial roots so that the top of the plant can be chopped off with its own rooted top. To do this wrap damp moss (you could even get this from a mossy lawn) around a bare bit of the trunk and cover with clingfilm. Make sure the moss remains damp and fairly quickly you'll find aerial roots sprouting inside.

There are numerous variegated cultivars:
Ficus benjamina 'Starlight' has large cream margins,
Ficus benjamina 'Golden King' has narrower creamy margins.
Ficus benjamina 'Reginald' has bright yellow and green variegation.

Ficus elastica, Rubber plant, comes from tropical Asia and is not the source of true rubber, but called this because it's such a bendy, rubbery thing. Huge specimens in India are manipulated so that the roots cover chasms and rivers until they form a living bridge. It has particularly free-flowing milky sap that will stain furniture, and thick, shiny, rubbery leaves. It prefers indirect, but bright conditions and it will not tolerate midday sun.

This is a fast-growing fig that is often sold as a single stem specimen when young; you should pinch back the growing tip to create a more branching habit. Cuttings of shoots 30cm (12in) or so will easily root in moist compost, so propagate if your plant decides it wants more space than you can offer. When they're happy these plants can turn into monsters rather quickly.

Ficus elastica 'Robusta' (pictured on page 108) has a strong, robust habit and branches well if pruned.
Ficus elastica 'Black Prince' has deep green foliage.
Ficus elastica 'Tineke' (pictured left) has white, pink and green variegation.

Ficus lyrata, Fiddle-leaf fig, comes from West Africa and is very similar in habit to the rubber plant with thick, pear-shaped leaves. Often this is sold as a young whip with a single stem; if you want a branching specimen (and you do because otherwise it'll become leggy with age) pinch out the growing tip to form branches. You can keep doing this every time the plant gets too big, pollarding back to the first cut if necessary to regenerate the plant. Remember to try and only prune in late winter to hide the scars. It prefers indirect light and can tolerate bright conditions but will not like direct midday light.

Ficus pumila, Creeping fig, is like the ivy plant of the fig world. This fig can look fantastic as it can be pruned and manipulated to make a lattice, but can also be grown as a hanging-basket or trailing shelf plant. It comes from east Asia, but has naturalised in parts of the United States and is often seen growing over stately homes in Italy. It can withstand fairly low temperatures and in a very sheltered courtyard garden in a city, it would survive outside as long as it doesn't get lower than 3°C/37°F. The species name, *pumila,* is derived from *pumilis* in Latin, meaning dwarf and refers to the small, thin, heart-shaped leaves. Treat this one like ivy, but never let it dry out completely as the whole thing shrivels up. It is exceptionally shade tolerant.

Ficus sagittata looks much like *F. pumila,* but is larger and with lance-shaped leaves. You are most likely to come across the variegated form, 'Variegata', which has irregularly edged, creamy margins.

Chlorophytum comosum, Spider plant, Asparagaceae

Ah the spider plant. I have such a soft spot for this ubiquitous beast. Too often you see tortured spider plants bravely soldiering on despite every bit of neglect the owner throws at them. We've probably all seen them growing with no natural light, no watering for months, then a drowning till the poor things dry out again. They often sit in pots with no drainage hole and if they are ever repotted in their lifetime, it's a miracle. Still, for all the tormented specimens, there are those that love their babies and repot and propagate so that every window is a cascade of leaves.

The spider plant has long been popular for the reasons above – love it or just tolerate it and still it grows. It has also been found to be incredibly effective at removing pollutants from the indoor environment, filtering out chemicals released from our computers, televisions, carpets and other manmade components to give us cleaner air to breathe.

Chlorophytum comosum is native to tropical and southern Africa. Here it is a forest-floor groundcover plant; the baby plantlets grow much as strawberries do on runners, so that they create thick patches. In the wild there are several intra-specific varieties, *C. comosum* var. *comosum*, *C. comosum* var. *bipindense* and *C. comosum* var. *sparsiflorum*. The last two have broader leaves than the first, as these grow deep in the shady Guineo–Congolian forest where larger leaves allow them to collect more light. The first grows on the margins of the forests and thus has thinner leaves. It's from this one that the cultivated species most likely comes from. Nearly all the wild forms are green; natural variegation is rare but does occur.

Unusually for rainforest species, spider plants can withstand a great deal of drought – although the forest floor of a rainforest is not as wet as you might expect, it is not bone dry either, yet the spider plant can go for months without watering. This is because it has fleshy, tuberous roots that can store a large amount of water for leaner times. Saying this, the best-grown plants enjoy regular watering and are misted every once in a while to keep the leaves shiny and clean.

Spider plants prefer shadier conditions but will grow in bright light though this tends to make the leaves rather bleached out or scorched. They will tolerate conditions as low as 4°C/39°F and as high as 30°C/86°F. To propagate, simply remove plantlets and insert them individually into small pots. Spider plants can make an attractive skirt around the base of large houseplants such as *Dracaena* and palms.

Chlorophytum comosum (pictured) has long, strap-like, green leaves with long, green branching flowering stalks (stolons) growing from a central crown. When less than a year old, 1–6 small, greenish-white flowers appear on the end of these wiry stems, and at the end of the inflorescence plantlets appear. The whole stolon will droop and eventually drop so that a plantlet touches the ground and advantageous roots appear. Sink these roots into a small pot full of damp compost next to the plant, and after 2–3 weeks the plantlet will have rooted happily in the compost and can be severed from the parent plant.

There are two common variegated varieties: **Chlorophytum comosum 'Vittatum'** has mid-green leaves with a broad central white stripe and white stolons. **Chlorophytum comosum 'Variegatum'** has dark green leaves with white margins and green stolons.

SPRING   SUMMER   AUTUMN   WINTER

Fittonia verschaffeltii, Nerve plant, Acanthaceae

This plant looks as if someone has taken chalk and drawn over the leaves, picking out every vein and midrib in detail. *Fittonia* is native to the Peruvian rainforest where it grows as groundcover on the moist forest floor. It does not like full sun and does not like drying out. If they dry out for a couple of days they 'faint', wilting dramatically, but are known to revive once rewetted. They may like things moist, but they dislike wet, which will rot their small root system very quickly. Get their conditions right and they are very easy to look after, but finding the right space in your house can take a few attempts. This one roots very easily from cuttings either in new compost or water, so if it's unhappy, grown leggy or rotting, try propagating it quickly for another round.

Fittonia verschaffeltii has white to deep pink veins on leaves 5–10cm (2–4in) long.

Fittonia verschaffeltii var. argyroneura has leaves traced in silver.

Jasminium polyanthum, Chinese jasmine, Oleaceae

This is the one that your grandmother loved and insisted a new one was bought each year, probably growing on a hoop, with its heady fragrance permeating the whole house. Originally from western China and Myanmar (formally Burma) where it is found growing in valleys, thickets and woodlands, it needs bright, but not direct light. It's particularly sensitive to direct sunlight in summer, which will cause the leaves to scorch and turn yellow. In winter, it can be moved to more direct light, which will aid flowering, and it can flower from winter through to late spring if happy. The trick to getting it to repeat flower is to prune it hard once the flowers are over; it may be necessary to untie it from its canes or metal support. Prune older stems back to within 8cm (3in) or so of the base, shorten any laterals back by a few centimetres and feed well over the summer, then it should bud up again for the following winter. It needs a minimum temperature of 3°C/37°F and it dislikes draughts, particularly when in bud. But don't keep it somewhere too hot, not over 15°C/59°F in winter – the best flowers seem to come from a cooler winter and temperate summer. *Jasminium polyanthum* should never be allowed to dry out completely. It doesn't take to having parched feet. This vine can grow up to 2m (6ft), but takes restricted life in a pot well; just keep twining it around itself and repot every few years.

SPRING · SUMMER · AUTUMN · WINTER

118

Tradescantia, Spiderworts, Commelinaceae

Tradescantia are native to the New World from Canada to Argentina and the West Indies, though they have naturalised in many other places. These are scramblers, climbers and trailers, though a few pretend to weakly stand upright, usually flopping about. They are mostly woodland plants, often growing in clumps. They have pretty white, pink, purple or blue flowers with three petals and six yellow anthers. As houseplants, they are best grown somewhere they can trail, either in a hanging basket or cascading from a shelf or wall planter. They tend to grow leggy, losing leaves along the stems so it's worth regularly pinching them back to encourage branching and cut them back hard if they become neglected. They are very easy to propagate –

cut a leaf off with a couple of centimetres (1in) or so of stalk and root in water or insert into a pot so that the leaf sits on the surface. Alternatively, propagate it by pegging down a plantlet-bearing leaf in compost until roots appear and then cut it off from the mother plant.

These are not frost hardy but can withstand temperatures as low as 0–4°C/32–39°F. They don't like direct sun and can be grown in deep shade or under fluorescent light, though cultivars with pronounced variegation will begin to revert to all green in low light levels. As their leaves are fleshy they can withstand periods of drought, only resuming growth when the conditions improve.

Tradescantia **'Green Hill'** has purple and green variegation.

Tradescantia fluminensis is native to South America where it grows as perennial groundcover, spreading across the ground with soft, hairless stems that root wherever a node touches the surfaces. The leaves are oval, dark green with pointed shiny and slightly fleshy tips. Flowers are white and there are numerous cultivars with variegated leaves. 'Quicksilver' has blue-green silver variegation and is fairly compact. 'Albovittata' has green leaves with cream and pale green variegation.

Tradescantia pallida, **Purple heart**, is native to Mexico where it scrambles along the ground. It has brittle, rather wayward purple stems with slightly hairy, lance-shaped leaves that are also purple and slightly fleshy. Pink flowers appear in summer.

Tradescantia zebrina, **Inch plant** (pictured right) is native to Mexico and Central America and has zebra-patterned leaves, the upper surface showing purple new growth. There are two broad, silver-coloured stripes to the outer edge of the leaf. The lower leaf surface is deep magenta and flowers are violet-purple. This is a trailing plant and works best in a basket or wide pot. The sap can cause irritation to some.

Peperomia, Pepper elder, Piperaceae

Peperomia are a huge genus with over 1000 different members, mostly small, compact epiphytes that grow on rotten wood in tropical rainforests, largely in tropical America although there are also a number of species from Africa. There are two main groups: small with stout, fleshy leaves from thick stems that are in rosette formation, or those with a more open bushy or trailing habit. The flowers are slightly insignificant yellow, white or brown conical or cordlike spikes. Leaves are smooth, fleshy and often oval or heart-shaped in green to grey-green with stripes, marbling, or bordered with pale green, red or grey. There are so many different cultivars and species floating around it would be impossible to list them all.

These are easy-going houseplants that don't mind shade or indirect light, but bright sunlight will scorch the leaves. This lot do well under artificial fluorescent light. The thing that bothers them the most is wet or soggy soil. They need light, well-draining soil and do best grown in shallow, wide pots. As they are epiphytes they do not have an extensive root system and if you grow them in a pot that is too big the pot will hold too much water and the roots will rot. They don't like too much fertiliser either. If white crusty deposits appear on the surface of the soil, this is usually a sign of excess salts from fertilisers. Flush the soil out with water and allow the pot to completely dry out again before repotting.

They love warm, humid conditions akin to the tropical rainforests that they grow in and need to be kept somewhere around 18–24°C/64–75°F.

In the winter when temperatures and light levels drop, water very sparingly from above, making sure that the crown does not get wet. This should prevent the plants from rotting off, which is the most common way to kill them.

Peperomia caperata is perhaps the most common species, known as the emerald ripple peperomia, native to Brazil. It is a compact bush-forming type with crinkled heart-shaped leaves puckered between the veins and narrow spikes of white flowers. It grows up to 20cm (8in) high and wide. *Peperomia caperata* 'Variegata' (pictured, in front of a *Peperomia* Rain Drop) has irregular, wide, silver-white margins on purple-brown background. The plant looks like burnished copper.

Peperomia griseoargentea, **Ivy leaf pepper**, is also native to Brazil. It has deeply veined heart-shaped, silver-grey leaves, tinted green or copper.

Peperomia obtusifolia is a low, bush-forming trailer that acts as groundcover in the Caribbean, Mexico and Florida. It has cupped, glossy, dark-green leaves often with prominent drip tips on short, very brittle red stems. This means the leaves easily break off but root easily in compost. There are numerous forms with gold, grey or cream variegations.

Peperomia scandens, **Cupid peperomia**, comes from Peru and is most often found in its variegated form 'Variegata' with pronounced heart-shaped leaves on trailing stems. It's good for hanging baskets or in front of larger specimens in big pots.

SPRING   SUMMER   AUTUMN   WINTER

Pilea, Urticaceae

These lovely little plants are in the same family as stinging nettles, not that you'd have any sense of that from the way they look. They are found through the tropics, subtropics and temperate zones and the majority of the species are succulent, shade-loving herbs. Unlike the other genus in this family, *Pilea* always have opposite leaves. They are very easy to grow, needing little love to thrive. Water sparingly, reduce watering over the winter, and allow the plants to dry out completely before watering again. Overwatering is the only way to kill them. Shade them from hot sun and that's about it.

Over time they can become a little leggy, but they are easy enough to propagate from leaf cuttings. Simply pinch a leaf off with its stalk and either start it in water or nestle it into damp soil. It will easily re-root. *Pilea* don't mind a bit of cold, happily surviving in 7–10 °C/44–50 °F, so are ideal for porches, conservatory or chilly windowsills (as long as they don't frost).

Pilea involucrata is known as the friendship plant because it is so easy to propagate. Just pinch off a leaf stalk and sit it in water or pop into damp soil. It is a bushy trailing plant with textured, dark green leaves with bronze undertones and light green edges. This one loves high humidity, making it good for a bathroom, and does well in terrariums. It is native to Central and South America. There are numerous cultivars often highlighting the copper, silver and bright green variegations. 'Moon Valley' is lime green and bronze. ' Norfolk' is deep bronze and silver.

***Pilea peperomioides*, Chinese money plant, Missionary plant** (pictured) has become a bit of an Instagram star and thus vastly popular. The round leaves are shiny, succulent, brilliant green on a long stalk. The leaves reach up to 10cm (4in) across. With age the plants become straggly and all the leaves crowd towards the top, so it's worth propagating to keep them looking neat and tidy. This plant is native to Yunnan province in southern China and was made popular in Europe by Agnar Espegren, a Norwegian missionary who took a cutting back home with him via India, which is how it got one of its common names.

Ferns

Ferns are old plants that first appeared on the earth 360 million years ago. They are vascular plants that reproduce via spores rather than seed or flowers, so they predate flowering plants. Ferns are most likely to be found growing in shady conditions. There are four types of fern habitat: moist, shady forests or woodlands, crevices in rock faces that are sheltered from full sun, acid wetlands and swamps, and tropical trees where they grow as epiphytes. They dislike full sun, draughts, dry air and temperature extremes. They like rich compost; many ferns grow in forest soils rich in leaf mould and decaying vegetable matter. They dislike drying out and the compost should be kept moist at all times. Although they dislike full sun, too little light can result in yellowing fronds. They prefer a position near a window that gets morning or afternoon sun during the summer. Direct light will scorch and burn the leaves. Ferns like to be repotted and the best depth of colour and frond size comes from a plant that is not in old, tired compost. This is best done in spring time and should only happen if you start to see roots coming out of the bottom of the pot. If the plant is tired, but doesn't have a great root mass, add a new layer of compost to the top of the pot instead. If necessary, scrap a little of the old compost off first. Ferns can be fed once a month during the growing season, but should be given a rest over winter.

Asparagus, Asparagus fern, Asparagaceae

These are not true ferns and are more closely related to lilies. The most famous member of this genus is edible asparagus, however none of the houseplants should be snacked on. The berries, in particular, are very toxic and may cause dermatitis if handled. However, male and female flowers appear on different plants and most houseplants are male plants. Asparagus ferns have what appear to be needle-like leaves. These are not true leaves but cladodes and are actually flattened stems or branches with green tissues scales that replace the function of leaves in performing photosynthesis. The true leaves are the tiny scales that appear where the cladodes meet the stem. They are mostly found growing in North and South Africa in moist areas where they naturally scramble and climb up other species via spines on the stem.

This lot are happiest grown in bright conditions with indirect light, a south-facing window will be too hot for them. Keep them moist throughout the growing season, starting to lessen watering from late autumn to late winter. Misting them in winter is helpful, especially if you are growing them near a radiator.

Asparagus setaceus, **Asparagus fern, Feathery fern** (pictured) is a bushy, feathery plant with tubers that grows up to 2.5m tall (8ft) if given a big enough pot. It has small white flowers that are followed by purple berries and is naturally climbing so could be trained to grow up a pole. The berries are toxic and should not be eaten – one to keep away from curious pets and small children. Grow in bright, indirect light and keep moist. Direct sun will scorch the leaves and too little light will cause the plant to go yellow and drop its 'needles'. It can survive short periods of drought.

Asparagus densiflorus, **Sprengeri Group, Emerald fern**, has feathery, somewhat leathery leaves that are upright at first, but gently arching and then becoming pendant with age. It suits being grown where it can cascade over a shelf or hanging basket. Repot in spring when it becomes rootbound and grow this one in bright, indirect light. It prefers temperatures above 10°C/50°F.

Adiantum, Maidenhair fern, Pteridaceae

Maidenhair ferns are such pretty, delicate things, all whimsy and flirt, fluttering their leaves at the slightest of breezes. They look like they'd be such easy, breezy company. They are not. They are the high-maintenance girlfriends of the houseplant world. Look away, pay attention to something else, disturb their microclimate and, god forbid, forget to water them a second later than they require it and they will shrivel up and die. Still I love them.

Firstly, repot them the minute you get them home. They hate dry feet and are often potted up in peat-based composts that are liable to dry out quickly. More compost will hold more water and thus there'll be less drying out. The roots must never dry out. Ever.

These houseplant ferns hail from the tropical Americas and are found in part shade in very humid conditions. The most successful plants I've owned lived in my bathroom and thrived in the steamy environment. Never try and grow them in full sun. Conversely, in full shade you'll find the fronds will lose their vitality.

If you have to sit them near a radiator or heat source, sit them in a tray of wet pebbles to keep humidity high. And of course they resent draughts. In truth, they resent most things; if you succeed consider yourself very good at this game. If the pot dries out, sit it in water until it's fully soaked. The name *Adiantum* is derived from the Greek *adiantos*, meaning unwetted and refers to the fact that the leaves are very good at repelling water. What you should take away from this is that watering from above can be tricky, more water will end up around the plant than in the pot.

The most common species is delta maidenhair fern, *Adiantum raddianum* (pictured) which grows to 30cm (1ft) high and won't be happy below 7°C/ 45°F. There are numerous cultivars; 'Micropinnulum' is like fairy dust and 'Fragrantissimum' by comparison looks like it's on steroids. Both are worth looking out for.

If your house is cold, go for the common maidenhair, *Adiantum capillus-veneris*, which will survive down to 1–2°C/32–35°F. It's native to southern U.S. through to Mexico, Central America and South America, where it likes to grow on moist, sheltered, shaded cliffs and gorges, often by streams or hot springs. If you get good at growing these try *Adiantum trapeziforme*, trapezoidal maidenhair, which comes from tropical rainforests in Central and South America. It needs a minimum of 10–13°C/50–55°F and has long, arching fronds with giant trapezoid pinnules (fern leaflets).

SPRING SUMMER AUTUMN WINTER

Asplenium, Shield fern, Aspleniaceae

There are two aspleniums worth growing indoors and many more that are suitable for outside. *Asplenium nidus,* the bird's-nest fern, and *Asplenium bulberiferum,* mother spleenwort, are both good, reliable houseplants for shady rooms but look so wildly different it's hard to imagine they are related.

Asplenium bulbiferum, **Mother spleenwort** or **Hen and chicks fern**, comes from Australia and New Zealand. The fronds are edible and are a traditional Maori vegetable, so if the zombie apocalypse comes and you get locked in your house, eat this one.

The 'hen and chicks' name comes from the small bulbils that grow on top of the fronds. Once these babies reach 5cm (2in) or so they drop off and, provided they land in moist soil, they grow into new ferns. Thus, if this plant likes your home you can amass a small forest of them. They work well as an understorey plant for large houseplants where they look very fine en masse. They will tolerate low light and can be grown in shade as long as the temperature is above 10°C/50°F. Low light and low temperatures will result in very small plants. They will not tolerate bright midday sun, which will scorch the leathery leaves. During the spring and summer months they'll require moderate watering; don't let the compost completely dry out. However, over the winter, water sparingly, keeping the compost just moist, but no more as they are liable to rot off at the base if too wet. It grows up to 75cm (32in) slowly.

Asplenium nidus (pictured) grows in rainforests in tropical southeast Asia, where they are epiphytical, living in niches of tree boughs, high up in the rainforest canopy. Unlike ground-dwelling plants, this lot derive all their nutrients from the air, rainwater or organic debris that collects in its environment. The organic debris and the mesh of roots act as a sponge to collect and hold water.

To keep a bird's-nest fern happy you need shady conditions; they grow under the canopy of tropical trees where they get at most filtered light, so they need good humidity and warmth (13°C/55°F minimum). Add patience to the mix and in time you can get an impressive plant with fronds that can grow up to several feet. Direct sun will scorch the shiny, lance-shaped leaves. This is the perfect plant for the bathroom as it will benefit from the humidity. Otherwise, grow in wet-pebbled trays. Fronds are delicate and damage easily, so avoid handling them. Don't fill the nest (the fronds rise from a crown with a central hollow that looks a little like a bird's-nest) with water, the whole thing will rot. Do make sure the compost never dries out.

Davallia tyermannii, Rabbit foot fern, Davalliaceae

Davallia is an epiphyte native to the Fiji islands where it grows off thick bark on tropical trees. The long rabbit's feet are furry aerial roots that sup up moisture and nutrients from the trees they grow off. Davallia make great houseplants because they actually don't mind relatively low humidity (but they won't like sitting near a radiator). They prefer indirect light and shady conditions. In a bright room you could sit them on the far side from the window and they'll still do well. Most often grown as hanging-basket plants, they will happily survive in a pot, just expect the furry feet to cover the pot. When repotting make sure never to bury the feet.

Nephrolepis exaltata, Boston or ladder fern, Nephrolepidaceae

This fern can grow into a magnificent creature, though you'd hardly know that from the tiny specimens sold in DIY stores. The elegant, arching fronds are best admired from a hanging basket or at least a pot stand where the fronds can cascade out from the centre of the plant.

The fronds are ladder-like, with alternate pinnae, but there are many cultivars with ruffled or lacy-edged forms if you like fancy things. This fern likes damp soil in a relatively humid atmosphere, but I've seen some impressive specimens that flout the rules because, if pushed to the edge, this one can survive a drought, though it often drops a lot of leaves in protest and takes some time to regain its looks. The trick is to pot it up every spring. The more room you give it the bigger it will grow – up to 90cm (3ft) across – so think stretch and keep potting. This fern is found on the ground in humid forests and swamps from South America to Florida, the West Indies, Polynesia and Africa where it thrives in shade, but indoors it does better with more light. It doesn't want direct sunlight, definitely not at midday, but bright filtered light will grow the best specimens. It's another good one for the bathroom because if humidity falls too low (it likes around 80 per cent relative humidity) it will start to scorch, particularly at the frond tips. I grow mine in my sitting room, which is hardly humid but I sit them in water-pebbled saucers and allow them to flop over the edge of a mantelpiece. If you are not growing them in a hanging basket, make sure you turn the plants regularly or they are liable to go bald on one side.

Ease off slightly on watering over the winter and cut back any fronds that become scorched to their base.

133

Platycerium bifurcatum, Staghorn fern, Polypodiaceae

I love a staghorn fern. They are the perfect houseplant. Weird, majestic and so easy to grow. You can't kill a staghorn fern and believe me I've tried. *Platycerium* are evergreen epiphytic ferns; they have two very distinct types of fronds and insignificant roots that are often hard to see. The fertile fronds look like stag or elk's antlers and are prominently forked. Brown spores form on these, which are the reproductive part of the fern. The infertile fronds are the small, flat, oval-shaped leaves that cover the root crown and form a shield. These eventually dry up and turn a very beautiful bronze colour. They wrap themselves around their tree-trunk support, generation after generation, until the plant is securely embracing its home. They'll do the same around a pot, corkboard or slab of bark. which are all used to grow them in the home. *Platycerium* species are largely native to southeast Asia, Polynesia and Australia. They don't all grow in the jungle; there's a species that grows on rocks in a desert in Australia.

Baby staghorns are often sold grouped together in a pot to make them look like a fuller plant. If you are careful you can separate each one and then either attach them to board or pot them on till they are big enough to be attached. Be very careful not to overwater them if you pot them on. Just mist the foliage and nothing more; if you water the compost they tend to easily rot off.

Platycerium bifurcatum is the easiest to get hold of, it has very showy, antler-like fronds that are covered in protective felt-like scales that look a lot like fuzzy felt. This is to protect the plant from drying out and harsh sunlight, both things that it doesn't like. The sterile fronds that wrap around whatever you decide to grow it on will eventually start to rot and amass debris. This is natural and how the plant is helping to feed itself. A new, bright green, sterile frond will grow out in front. Staghorns can grow to an immense size, just wrapping themselves endlessly around their own dead fronds. The best trick to work out whether they need water or not is to feel behind the infertile fronds; they should never completely dry out. I like to mist the sterile fronds so that the white scales go translucent. This can be done every few days and the plant will be blissfully happy. If it completely dries out it's best to dunk the whole plant in cold water for a few minutes. Staghorns can live outside in the summer and will even take a few fairly chilly nights. These ferns do not like to be left in full sun, preferring bright filtered light akin to the light they'd receive in the canopy of a tree.

Platycerium superbum is much larger than *bifurcatum* and really has to be grown on bark or corkboard to look its best. If you buy a staghorn fern in a pot, at some point you'll need to transfer it onto bark or a corkboard. To do this, you'll have to gingerly unwrap it from the pot, which might damage it a little, but it will recover if you're kind to it. Then attach it to the board using fishing wire. Do not be tempted to use copper wire. It might look cool, but the plant will be deeply upset by the copper. Carefully wrap the fishing wire around the sterile frond and the board until it's secure. Eventually new sterile fronds will cover up the wire. If suspended, a staghorn fern will grow into an immense globe – something to aim for!

136

Phlebodium pseudoaureum, Virginia blue fern, Blue
rabbit foot fern, Polypodiaceae

This has very attractive glaucous foliage that's not often
found in houseplants which tend to be deeper green.
Found growing naturally from Mexico to tropical South
America, it's tougher looking than it might appear, and
is another epiphytic type, with creeping, densely hairy,
red rhizomes bearing fronds. Each frond persists for one
or two years then dies off. It's not easy to get hold of this
fern, but well worth it. It's fairly hardy too, so if you're
not into heating your house over the winter, this is the
houseplant for you. Just don't overwater those rhizomes
because they'll rot off quickly. Saying that, it doesn't
like drying out, either. Keep it in a cool room and the
compost will remain moist, a north-facing bathroom or
kitchen is ideal. Stick it near a radiator and you'll likely
lose this one. It doesn't mind bright light, but direct
midday sun will scorch the leaves. If you repot it, try
and use an orchid potting mix with plenty of bark in
it so the soil is freedraining. This isn't a fern that will
need repotting regularly; leave it be unless you find the
leaves are yellowing, then it's time to repot.

Pteris cretica, Cretan brake fern, Ribbon fern,
Pteridaceae

This is a very slow-growing evergreen fern with long,
elegant feather-like fronds, Pteris comes from the Greek
word for feather and cretica, from Crete, though it has
roamed further afield than its name suggests. It's an Old
World tropical and subtropical fern found in Europe,
Asia and Africa. It does well in shady conditions and
appreciates some humidity, so it's another one for the
bathroom. What it most likes is to have cool roots, so
do not sit it above a radiator. It does best in clay pots
sitting in a saucer of pebbles. Water regularly during
the spring and summer, slightly reducing this during
winter as the cool, moisture-loving roots will rot off if
they sit in water over the winter. If the fronds scorch or
just look a little tired, cut them back to the base and it
will rejuvenate, albeit slowly if you decide to cut it back
in winter.

The variegated variety, *Pteris cretica* var. *albolineata*
(pictured), has greyish fronds with white central
patches down the centre of each leaflet. It's interesting
looking, but I think I prefer the understated elegance of
the species.

Streptocarpus, Cape primose, Gesneriaceae

Streptocarpus have leaves that look very similar to primrose and flowers that are almost orchid like. The most common types are bred from *Streptocarpus saxorum* and have a rosette of thick, leathery, deep green leaves. They are found growing in ravines and valleys of the Drakensberg mountains in South Africa, where they grow in moist soil in shaded conditions. They like indirect light and are perfect for north-northwest and east-facing windows. Too much sun will burn the leaves and shade the flowers. Although they like humid conditions it is important not to overwater them. The soil should be dry to the touch between watering. If underwatered the plant will wilt, but will revive quickly with a little love. Too much food or water will give you large, dramatic leaves and no pretty flowers. Water less in winter and don't feed them. It's very natural for the old leaves to turn yellow and die back; trim them off as this happens. As spring unfurls start to water them more and repot each spring into a slightly larger pot. If you feed them regularly throughout the growing season from spring to autumn, you will have a continual display of flowers. Rot can happen at the base of the leaves. Trim off any diseased material – usually this is a sign that you are watering too much. There are numerous hybrids and cultivars with flowers from deep purple to blue, pink and white.

Begonias

My love for begonias runs deep. Begonias have long been seen by a certain sort of horticultural tribe as deeply naff. Bedding begonias for summer displays certainly test the standards of taste, but indoor, tropical begonias are far from this. They are easy friends with luxurious, exotic, often strange and rather brilliant leaves. They can be stately or short, fragile and yet tough, or fragile and not so tough. Their flowers are pretty, but you'll rarely write home about them. They are a doddle to propagate and a joy to do so and you will start with one and, before you know it, you'll be producing an orchestra and filling every available spot.

Begonias are a large gang with many hybrids. All of them are native to moist subtropical and tropical climates in South and Central America, Africa and Asia. Most species are forest understorey plants and require bright shade; few will tolerate full sun. They are perfect for north- and east-facing windows that receive little or no sun. Ideally they need to be in a constant temperature and dislike, say, a cool morning and a hot afternoon so in south-facing rooms it's best to keep them away from the window, a couple of feet in with perhaps taller plants in front of them to protect them from direct light.

For the best foliage colour keep red types in bright indirect light and silver types in a lower light intensity. Silver-leaved types can be grown quite successfully in rooms with no natural light, but at some point they will need a rotation to a window with natural light.

For the best growth, they need a minimum temperature of 15°C/59°F, though some can go as low as 5°C/41°F. While the plants are actively growing from late winter to early autumn they should be kept moist and should be fed from early spring to midsummer. Over the winter they can dry out a little but not totally. They will tell you immediately if they are too dry as the ends of the leaves will curl up and turn crispy. It's easy to overwater begonias and rot them, so make sure that the compost never stays wet; moist, yes, but not so that the plant is sitting in water in the saucer.

You can eat begonia flowers; they are sour and taste like lemon juice or sorrel leaves. Try adding them to salads as a pretty acid note to cut through salad-dressing oil.

Rhizomatous begonias are the largest group of begonias. They grow from stems, rhizomes, that grow along the surface of the soil. You could say they recline and, as they do this, the stems put out new roots where they touch the soil. Like most begonias, they are grown for their interesting foliage. There are brilliant greens, blacks, silver and browns, a whole group that swirl like a snail's shell, many with ruffled edges and some with interesting hairs. They nearly all bloom after a period of short days, so will do so in winter and spring. The flowers are small, but surprisingly charming, particularly as they appear when little else wants to flower. This lot don't mind quite deep shade and can grow in rooms without natural light. They should be

allowed to dry out a little between watering. Getting water on the leaves isn't a particular problem, but they are quite susceptible to a mould called botrytis and this is always made more problematic by cool temperatures. During winter, make sure that the compost is not kept too wet, as cool, damp conditions will exacerbate the problem.

The black types will revert to green if conditions are too shady. The colour can vary widely in different light conditions so play around and see what suits an individual best. They are very easily propagated from stem and rhizome cuttings.

Begonia **'Black Fang'** (pictured on page 144) has black, shallowly lobed leaves on red hair-covered stems. It looks very similar to 'Black Velvet'. Both are hungry plants and should be fed regularly through the growing season.

Begonia **'Escargot'** (pictured right) is the swirliest of all swirly begonias and looks like a snail's shell. Leaves grow up to 30cm (12in) on red, hairy stems and it can grow up 50cm (20in) tall. This plant will drop all of its leaves if it dries out, but conversely will rot if too wet so requires dedicated watering. The silver colouring on the leaves is most prominent if grown in shade.

Begonia **'Fireworks'** has strongly veined leaves with dark centres, purple edges and a pink and silver zone. It is very much on the edge of tasteful, but deliciously so.

Begonia **'Marmaduke'** has toothed, slightly bubbly, pale green leaves with brownish markings. The stem and edges of the leaves are hairy. It's a strange and rather beguiling thing; the leaves grow up to 20cm (8in) across and it has pale white flowers on tall stems.

Begonia **'Raspberry Swirl'** is an even pinker version. The old low-growing varieties, *Begonia* **'Merry Christmas'** and *Begonia* **'Happy New Year'**, are very similar. Both are very striking, with a clear zone of black, silver and green with a somewhat pink tinge to 'Merry Christmas' and no spots.

Begonia **'Orange Rubra'** is an upright sub-shrub with green, cane-like stems and bright green, angel-wing leaves with paler undersides. The leaves are often spotted when young. It grows to 1m (3ft), with leaves up to 15cm (6in). Known for its bright orange-red flowers, as with many begonias, the male flowers open first, followed by females on more hanging bunches. This is a cross between *Begonia dichroa* from Brazil and the hybrid *Begonia* 'Coral Red'. It's good in hanging baskets as the stems have a tendency to recline when they get long.

143

Begonia x *corallina* **'Lucerna'** is the largest cane type, growing up to 2m (6ft) if you give it a big enough pot. The leaves reach 15cm (6in) long. They're olive-green, angel-wing shaped with white spotting above and reddish beneath. Flowers are a rich rose-pink; the males open first on a spreading inflorescence and the females later in large hanging bunches. It's a hybrid of *Begonia coccinea* from Brazil.

Begonia luxurians, **Palm-leaf begonia** (pictured left on page 143) comes from the tropical forest floor in Brazil. It has thick, red, fleshy, cane-like stems, with large palmate leaves and white, frothy flowers in summer if it has grown big enough. It grows to 1.5m (4ft 6in), its leaves up to 30cm (1ft) across. Keep potting this one up and let it grow to its full size. It needs a minimum of 5°C/41°F and, in my experience, needs watering year-round. You can keep it outside in summer months.

Begonia maculata **'Wightii'** is an upright sub-shrub that grows to 2m (6ft) tall with time. It has olive-green, white-spotted leaves shaped like angel's wings, crimson beneath. The leaves are up to 15–25cm (6–9in) long. The flowers are white; the male ones open first and then the female ones, which form more of a hanging bunch. It is native to Brazil, specifically near Rio de Janiero, where it grows on mossy logs and rocks on the forest floor. It needs a minimum of 5°C/41°F.

Begonia rex comes from China and was introduced to Europe in 1858. The leaves are heart-shaped with silver-green zones near the margins. It became a huge hit and was soon crossed with other rhizomatous begonias. These hybrids are known as rex begonias. Most varieties make small, stemless plants. They require shade all year around and prefer high humidity in the summer. They hate wet soil and need a compost that is very open, so sand or bark should be added to houseplant compost when repotting.

Cane-stemmed begonias have. thick, fleshy stems that look like bamboo canes, with distinct nodules along the stem. They are easy to propagate from stem-tip cuttings in water or compost. They can grow very leggy and the easiest way to maintain healthy stock is to regularly take cuttings.

Aspidistra elatior, Cast-iron plant
Asparagaceae

Aspidistra comes from the Asparagus family and earns its name cast-iron plant for its extreme tolerance of neglect. You can irregularly water it, forget about it, allow it to dry out to the brink of death and then give it some attention and, like a faithful hound, it will get on with life. It is also very hardy for a houseplant; it can be grown outside in the shade as long as conditions don't drop below -5°C/23°F and is excellent groundcover for very dry shade – for example, under coniferous trees.

It looks stately in a copper pot and you can pour endless amounts of booze from parties on it and it still soldiers on. Perhaps because it could take draughty houses and pollution from coal and gas fires it became a middle-class Victorian favourite and there are numerous black and white photos of great, handsome plants in front living rooms. It's sadly dropped a little popularity and, although it does little more than provide strapping green leaves (the flowers are tiny and dull), it is a very good houseplant for cold, dark rooms. It will never outshine a majestic pot, which I think is the way to treat this one – buy the best, most handsome pot you can and let that do the talking.

Aspidistra elatior comes from China and southern Japan. Despite its drought tolerance, it is a groundcover plant found in areas with fairly high rainfall, in forests and under shrubs. It does not like direct sunlight, which will scorch the leaves. A common houseplant in Japan, it was also commercially used to create the divisions in the compartment of a bento box. It rarely needs feeding, but be kind and feed at least once in the growing season for a fresh flush of new leaves. Don't let it sit in water or the plant will rot. It's worth poking holes into the compost every once in a while with a chopstick as it likes open compost to thrive.

It can collect a lot of house dust and a shower in the bath will help keep the leaves shiny and the stomata unblocked. Just because you can torture an aspidistra doesn't mean that you should!

Aspidistra elatior 'Asahi' means morning sun and has brown new growth that eventually fades to deep green.

Aspidistra elatior 'Hoshi-zora' means starry sky and the leaves are lightly spotted.

Aspidistra 'Okame' is a variegated form with creamy, white stripes to the margins of the leaf.

147

148

Medinilla magnifica, Rose grape, Melastomataceae

Magnificent is a truly appropriate name for this wonderful plant. In the Philippines it grows as an epiphyte in the fork of large trees and for this reason is sometimes known as the Philippines orchid. However, it is very suited to life in a pot and makes an excellent houseplant. It is known as the rose grape thanks to its panicles of flowers that look like rose-pink grapes when they are in bud. These hang down underneath the umbrella of the thick, leathery leaves and appear off hanging, tiered bracts. It looks like someone's fantasy rather than a real plant. The flowers appear from late spring to summer, but even when not in flower it looks very handsome, thanks to its large, paired, deep glossy green leaves. House it in a large pot on a shelf or somewhere the flowers can hang.

As it is an epiphyte it is used to being shaded from direct sunlight by the tree canopy and won't like sitting in hot, bright conditions or its leaves will scorch. In the winter, when temperatures may drop, slightly lessen the water requirements so that the plant doesn't rot, but don't stop watering. Allow the plant to just about dry out between watering and mist or sit it in a tray full of pebbles and water to keep humidity high. Feed throughout the growing season, from late spring to the end of summer. Repot every couple of years. This plant will grow up to 90cm (3ft) tall and wide if given a big enough pot.

Schefflera, Umbrella tree Araliaceae

Schefflera in their native habitats grow to enormous trees with huge inflorescences full of nectar-rich flowers that last for many months, making them important pollinator plants. However, they rarely get to a size where they can flower in a house where they are grown for their handsome stature and interesting foliage. They need to be shaded from hot, direct sun and resent cold draughts. You can bonsai a *schefflera*, which tells you that these are tough plants. They have become popular houseplants because they can grow in low light levels and will tolerate poor growing conditions and erratic watering. Be nice though and water regularly, making sure that the water drains right the way through the pot. If yellow leaves drop regularly you are overwatering it.

Schefflera actinophylla can reach 12m (40ft) in the wild. It has light olive leaves that are composed of 5–16 leaflets up to 30cm (12in) long. It needs to grow in a minimum of 10°C/50°F. It is native to New Guinea, Queensland and the Northern Territory of Australia where it grows in tropical rainforests, often as an epiphyte on rocks.

Schefflera arboricola, **the Parasol plant**, is the smaller version of *S. actinophylla*. It is native to Taiwan and Hainan where it often grows as an epiphytic shrub or large liana (woody vine), climbing into the canopy of other trees to flower. It has more leaflets than *S. actinophylla*, up to 11 per leaf. It prefers a shady position with no draughts and likes to be moist year round, but never wet. Don't let this plant sit in water as it's a common way to kill it. There are numerous variegated varieties, often in cream and gold.

Calathea, Marantaceae

Calathea is a large genus of leafy tropical plants from the Americas. They are lower-storey plants from damp, swampy forest floors and are used to periodic flooding, so they are the perfect plant for an erratic waterer. *Calathea allouia* is grown for its tubers that are eaten much like potatoes. They are almost impossible to find as a houseplant, but if you stumble across one it would make an interesting edible addition. *Calathea* have earnt their place in our homes because of their extraordinarily beautiful tropical foliage. There are forms with silvers, whites, chevrons, white lines, pink lines (*Calathea ornata* pictured), stripes and splashes. Often they look as if someone has painted them. Sometimes the breeding goes a little over the top and they look like a seventies' nightmare, but grouped together they make a majestic display and are so easy to look after that, if you're looking for a big houseplant, these are the ones for you. The leaves are easy to identify, though not dissimilar from *Ctenanthe*. The leaves have a long leaf stalk and are paddle-shaped, often with wavy margins and some species have coloured flowers as well. The back of the leaves are typically dark purple, the colour allowing the plants to absorb low light. These plants are truly adapted to thrive in very filtered, dingy conditions. The leaves are tough and have traditionally been woven into small containers or used to wrap foodstuff. *Calathea* like warm rooms, 16°C/60°F and above. They do not like direct sun and their leaves scorch easily. They are best grown in shade or indirect light. They love high humidity; sitting the pot on a saucer filled with gravel will help them, or grouping plants together to create a microclimate. Repotting every year will significantly improve the vigour of your plants, but if you're fairly neglectful they'll still survive. Leaf rolling is a sign that the plant is desperately thirsty, but the leaves drawing themselves in, particularly in the evening, is a sign that it's time for bed. These leaves move around a lot as they readjust themselves to get the best light. Don't be surprised if they wave at you.

Calathea crocata, **Eternal flame**, gets its name from its yellow and orange flowers that last for 2–3 months at a time. It comes from Brazil, where sadly it's rather rare due to environmental destruction of its habitat. The leaves are dark green and slightly wrinkled with dark purple to purple-brown undersides. It grows up to 60cm (2ft) tall.

Calathea lancifolia, **Rattlesnake plant**, is also native to Brazil; it has slender pale green leaves marked with dark blotches above and deep purple below. It grows to 60–75cm (12–18in).

Calathea majestica 'Albo lineata' has upright, dark green leaves with pronounced white stripes along the veins on both sides of the leaf. The underside of the leaf is purple.

Calathea makoyana, **Peacock plant**, has very striking leaves with papery, almost see-through markings that make it look a bit like a stained-glass window.

Calathea rufibarba, **Furry feather**, has dark, glossy green leaves with a deep purplish-brown underside. It gets its common name because the leaves and stems are covered with tiny hairs, giving it a velvety texture.

Calathea zebrina, **Zebra plant**, as the name suggests, has bright green leaves with symmetrical marks that run parallel along the leaves. The undersides are purple.

Ctenanthe, Marantaceae

Ctenanthe are most often found in Brazil. Much like *Calathea* they have highly attractive, often variegated leaves. Again, they have long stalks and paddle-shaped leaves that also like to move around in the same way as *Calathea*. This movement is known as nyctinasty and is a response to darkness. The leaves will close up as the night draws in and wave about in the morning to catch the best rays. They need a minimum of 16°C/60°F and don't like getting a chill. They need dappled light, they will scorch easily in full sun, and also require humidity. Stand in a tray of wet gravel or group plants together to create a microclimate. A warm bathroom is ideal if you have space.

Ctenanthe oppenheimiana, **Never-never plant**, is very elegant with long leaf stalks. It grows to 75cm (30in) tall with silver markings on a dull green background and a purple underside to the leaf.

Ctentanthe oppenheimiana 'Tricolor' has more pronounced markings. Leaves are heavily variegated in cream and silver-green with light red undersides.

Maranta, Marantaceae

This is another group in this tribe and, again, it looks very similar to both *Ctenanthe* and *Calathea*. There is one edible species *Maranta arundinaceae*, West Indian arrowroot, that comes from the West Indies and is an important, very ancient food crop. However, as a houseplant, *Maranta leuconeura* is the main species grown. *Maranta* need a minimum of 15°C/60°F, but are much happier around 21°C/ 70°F and like indirect, filtered light. In the tropics, they grow as groundcover in moist, shady areas of the rainforest floor. If you keep these plants at cooler temperatures, water sparingly as they will easily rot.

Maranta leuconeura, **Prayer plant** (pictured), gets its name because the leaves draw up together each night, like two hands in prayer, lying flat again during the day. It is native to Brazilian rainforests and grows up to 30cm (12in). The leaves have distinctive dark green markings down the middle of the plant.

Maranta leuconeura **var. erythroneura**, **Herringbone plant**, has strong red veining on dark green leaves.

Araceae

These are easily distinguished as a family as the leaves are nearly always heart- or arrow-shaped with prominent drip tips at the end. The drip tip is the pointed bit and usually indicates that the plant grows in a moist or wet habitat. Its function is to draw moisture away from the leaf surface. This has two effects: firstly the leaf doesn't stay damp in conditions where moulds would grow quickly, and the tip drips water to the roots. Rainforests may be wet, but the amount of water that reaches the forest floor can quickly evaporate to humidity, so the plants in these conditions make every effort to direct the water to where it's needed. On the whole Araceae family prefer indirect light.

Alocasia, Araceae

Alocasia is a striking genus in the Araceae family. These are lush foliage plants found in tropical and subtropical forests from Asia to Australia and have large, often shiny, striking leaves. They like warm conditions, around 16°C/60°F and above, but can survive if it's a bit cooler in bright but indirect light. If grown in too shady conditions the leaf petiole (the stalk) will elongate and the plant will become very floppy, but direct sunlight quickly scorches and bleaches the leaves. They like high humidity and to be kept damp, but it is easy to rot the underground rhizome if growing conditions are too wet and cool, so water sparingly. Given a big enough pot, the underground rhizome will spread to a considerable clump in time.

Alocasia x amazonica (pictured) is a horticultural hybrid with arrow-shaped leaves that are deep, dark, highly polished green with wavy margins. The veins and leaf margins are picked out in white markings and the back of the leaves are purple. It looks cartoonish, but in a brilliant, shiny way. It grows to 60cm (2ft) high. It prefers indirect, bright light and needs to be watered sparingly over the winter, allowing it to almost dry out between waterings.

Alocasia cuprea, **Jewel alocasia**, is a thing of great beauty. It comes from the rainforests of Borneo and has huge, almost oval leaves with deep recessed veins so that the areas between appear raised. The leaf is dark green with the raised areas almost grey-green and so shiny the whole thing appears metallic. The leaf undersides are purple. It prefers indirect, bright light and needs to be allowed to almost dry out between waterings, particularly in the winter.

Alocasia cuprea 'Blackie' (pictured) is deep brownish-purple. It is very sensitive to direct sunlight.

Alocasia macorrhiza, **Elephant's ear**, **Giant taro** is found growing in Sri Lanka and Malaysia where it easily reaches 1.8m (5ft) tall, but it needs a huge pot to do this indoors. The leaves are glossy green with prominent margins and can grow huge, up to 90cm (3ft) long with stems the same length. The tuber is edible when processed (not that I can imagine anyone uprooting their houseplant for that). Again, it wants that tricky thing of good light, but not direct light and it does tend to grow leggy and flop over indoors. Still if you can make it happy, it's well worth growing.

Caladium, Araceae

Angel's wings, *Caladium*, are another group of foliage plants with heart-shaped leaves from the tropics in the Americas and West Indies. I say another, but I don't mean it dismissively, just that the Araceae family is huge and there are many beauties. Most of the houseplant Caladiums are hybrids of *Caladium bicolor* and come with leaves and stalks in an array of brilliant and bright hues. The leaves are very thin and the pale colours can seem translucent, particularly if there's white variegation in there. These plants cling to conditions from home and need hot conditions to thrive, 21–24°C/70–75°F in the day and 16–18°C/60–65°F at night. They will give up the ghost very quickly if you sit them in a cold draught. And, like many other tropical foliage plants, they want bright conditions but not direct sunlight, which will quickly scorch the leaves. Often you'll find that they go dormant in the winter, dying back to their underground corms. You can keep the pots at cooler temperatures during this period, around 16°C/60°F, and keep watering down to a minimum, perhaps once or twice during the winter, just so that the corms don't shrivel up.

SPRING   SUMMER   AUTUMN   WINTER

Aglaonema, Chinese Evergreen, Araceae

Aglaonema are grown mostly for their foliage, which is often dark green with silvery markings. They love the shade and are easily scorched and bleached by the sun. They are perfect for a room with Roman blinds because they love filtered light, or use larger plants to cast shade over them. They respond well to regular potting on and feeding throughout spring and summer and prefer some humidity. A saucer with pebbles in it counteracts central heating in winter or high temperatures in

summer. You can cut back old, untidy plants in spring to about 5cm of the base and they will resprout.

Aglaonema commutatum is native to the Philippines and has dark green leaves with silver markings.
Aglaonema **'Malay Beauty'** is a striking combination of deep green, mottled white, cream and green.
Aglaonema **'Red'** or sometimes **'Siam Red'** has brilliant, bright red-tinted leaves with white and green markings.

Zamioculcas zamiifolia, ZZ plant, Araceae

The ZZ plant is a recent houseplant – it only really came on the scene in 2000. It's not new to the world; *Zamioculcas zamiifolia* has been around for a very long time but it's very slow growing and, although easy enough to propagate, each leaflet will root. It takes an age to get from there to a number of feathers, which is what the leaves are known as. The more feathers the more desirable the plant.

The ZZ plant comes from the foothills of the East African highlands, where it grows in a number of different situations – in rocky grasslands, on the margins of tropical highland forests and in other rocky places. It tends to like a little shade. In rocky grasslands, where there is usually a rainy season and a dry season, it will go dormant, waiting until the moisture appears again. You need to know this because it is often said that the plants are indestructible and they are, but there's a difference between, 'I'm not dead, I'm just hiding in my roots' and a plant you want to look at. You can get away with not watering and causing it to think there's a perpetual dry season at hand, but you are growing this one for its fine glossy leaves, thick, healthy petioles and its striking ladder-like feathers. Water it, regularly, allowing it to just start to dry out between waterings and you will have a lovely-looking plant. In winter, you can slow down on the watering because the low light levels means it's slowing down on growth too.

In brighter conditions, it will survive a south-facing window as long as there's no direct light scorching it; you will have to water more frequently. I think the ZZ plant is best grown in indirect, slightly shady conditions though, it certainly won't mind a north-facing window if it's warm enough. Ideally it likes 18–22°C/64–71°F,

159

but can survive around 10°C/50°F. It just won't put on much growth below 15°C/59°F.

If the leaves start to turn yellow, this is a sign that it is being watered too much. If the leaves drop, it is going dormant. It can withstand a dry season because it has thick, fleshy rhizomes which will store water and nutrients to keep the plant ticking over. If your plant is healthy and in a plastic pot and it decides in needs more room you will know as the roots can burst a pot open.

Spathiphyllum, *Peace lily,* Araceae

Peace lilies hail from tropical South America and the name *Spathiphyllum* is derived from the Greek for leaf – *spathe*, with *phyllum* being another name for leaf. A white spathe surrounds the protruding flower cluster, known as a spadix. The spathe resembles a pure white hanky. These plants tend to grow in swampy fields or along the margins of the rainforest in boggy conditions or on river banks, often growing in several inches of water. This is one houseplant that can drink a lot but doesn't want to sit in soggy conditions for days on end, as this reduces the available oxygen in the soil and causes conditions to become anaerobic.

These plants can withstand very low light levels but they don't necessarily like them. If you want the flowers to bloom they need bright, but not direct light. The spathe unfurls a brilliant pure white; after 10 days or so it will start to turn a pale green, but will persist for at least a month. After that the whole flower stalk should be cut back.

The leaves are deep, glossy green and will scorch in bright light. Peace lilies should be allowed to dry out between watering, but not allowed to wilt, which will cause those lovely deep green leaves to yellow very quickly. These plants are not huge fans of tap water, particularly heavily chlorinated waters, so it's always a good idea to let tap water sit for several hours in a wide-mouthed jug so that the chlorine can evaporate a little. They are also a little temperamental about very cold water, so allowing the water to rise to room temperature is another added benefit. If this seems like a lot of effort for such an ordinary houseplant, get in the habit of refilling the watering can when you have finished watering so that it is already prepared when it comes to watering again. Nestle the can between plants and it will also keep the atmosphere a little humid as it slowly evaporates.

If peace lilies are a little needy about water requirements, they make up for this by having very low fertility needs. Over-fertilising will burn the roots, so only feed once a summer. These plants do best around 16–20°C/60–68°F with a night-time temperature as low as 10°C/50°F, but no lower or growth will slow considerably.

They do best when slightly potbound, but that doesn't mean keeping them in a small pot, where they will dry out too quickly; just don't put them in too large a pot when it comes to moving up to the next size container. Repot in late winter or early spring if possible. Like any highly glossy leaves, house dust will show up on them and they benefit from being showered with lukewarm water to keep them clean. Don't use houseplant cleaning spray, it's horrid stuff. Instead, use a damp cloth. These plants rarely suffers from pests; if any do appear you'll find them on the underside of the leaves which are less glossy.

Peace lilies are perhaps a little old-fashioned, but there are not many houseplants that can bloom profusely in moderate light levels. They also have the useful ability to remove volatile organic compounds, such as solvents, from the indoor atmosphere so they should still be firm favourites for the home.

Most *Spathiphyllum* sold are hybrids with considerably larger spathes than you'd find in the wild, or have some form of variegation. *Spathiphyllum wallisii* is the most widely available species. It comes from Colombia and has dark green leaves and ovate, white flowering spathes up to 15cm (6in) long, each with a slender cream spadix. *S. wallisii* can be grown in a tropical aquarium though never submerged in water as it is not a true aquatic plant. It also works well in terrariums.

SPRING   SUMMER   AUTUMN   WINTER

Epipremnum aureum, Pothos vine or Devil's ivy, Araceae

Devil's ivy has earnt a reputation for being impossible to kill, and it is very, very tough. It comes from Moorea Island in French Polynesia and is a large evergreen vine that can grow up to 20m (70ft) tall with aerial clinging roots that allow it to climb tropical forest trees. In the right conditions and given enough room this will grow in to a rampant vine. I have seen them cascade down tall bookcases and clamber across the curtains in a bid to take on new ground.

The vines can be grown in low light levels and hot sun may scorch the leaves. They tolerate dryness, but not overwatering which causes rot. Dry air from radiators can cause brown markings on the leaves.

There are numerous cultivars around, the species has heart-shaped leaves that can grow up to 30–45cm (12–18in) long, though in a small pot the leaves rarely reach more than 15cm (6in). The leaves are deep green marbled with creamy yellow marking. In some cultivars, this marbling is yellow, gold or silver.

Grow them in a minimum temperature of 10–13°C/50–55°F and they will need watering all year round.

163

Monstera deliciosa, Swiss cheese plant, Araceae

Monstera deliciosa, the Swiss cheese plant, gets its name from its large, lobed leaves that have Gruyère cheese holes in them. Not all the leaves have holes; in fact there is a correlation between the height of the leaf – this plant is a climber – and how holey it is. The higher up the leaf, the more holes it will have, in order to facilitate two things: to allow more light and more water to the leaves below. This sort of pattern of holes is known as fenestration. The Swiss cheese plant is native to tropical rainforests of southern Mexico and Panama, although it has been introduced into many other tropical areas, where at times it has become a little invasive.

The seedlings like to start life in the darkest areas until they find a tree to climb, when they start to grow towards the light. Small, young plants like to grow in shade and will happily grow even in artificial light. As the plants mature they want more light, though it's not until they are very mature that they can withstand direct sun. Plants grown in too much light often look stunted and the leaves yellow. As this is a plant that likes to climb, skylights are ideal and this makes a great plant for stairwells. The happier the plant, the larger the leaves grow, reaching 60cm (2ft) across when mature. These plants are often sold with a coir or moss pole in the middle of the pot; sometimes the roots are already well into the pole. The ideal is that you keep the pole moist as *Monstera* loves the high humidity that you'd expect in a tropical rainforest. As the plant grows you'll find it clinging to the pole.

With age the plant gets longer and longer aerial roots that not only help to prop it up as it grows, but also help to feed it. These roots like to search for pockets of leaf mould often found in the crucks of branches, at which point the aerial roots will sprout fibrous feeding roots. If aerial roots appear on your plant, try and push them back into the soil so they can feed, or attach them to a moss pole or a moss bed in the pot's saucer. You can cut off the aerial roots without any harm to the plant. If your *Monstera* threatens to take over, you can prune it back hard in spring with little detriment to the plant.

The *deliciosa* refers to the truly delicious fruit, somewhere between pineapple and fruit salad sweets. Sadly, it rarely fruits indoors, though you may get to see the cream coloured flower spathes if the plant matures enough.

Philodendron, Araceae

Philodendron are the second largest genus in the Araceae family and are a diverse bunch. Some philodendrons (the name means tree-loving) have heart-shaped leaves, some are deeply lobed and there are even fairly succulent ones. Some are epiphytes and others are hemiepiphytic, meaning that they start life usually high up in the canopy of other tropical rainforest trees as an epiphyte but eventually grow long, thick, fleshy aerial leaves that touch the forest floor to obtain nutrients.

The philodendrons I think of nearly always have big, very tropical-looking leaves at least 30cm (12in) long and they come from deep in the interior of the rainforest where they thrive in humid, very warm conditions in the deep shade of the tree canopy where even the epiphytes high in the trees only receive filtered, dappled light. This is one genus that can sit at the far side of a north-facing room and thrive if its heat and humidity requirements are met. In hot sun the leaves will typically scorch and turn yellow. Happy plants will often send out aerial roots to seek moisture, and sitting these plants in a deep saucer with pebbles or leca to improve humidity is a good idea. A happy, handsome philodendron is quite something.

If a plant needs pruning, cut to a node – the tips of shoots often easily root in water or damp compost and make fun giant cuttings. If the tip of the plant has aerial roots the plant can be cut off just below a node with a root or two and potted on.

Although plants can be grown at temperatures as low as 10°C/30°F, new growth will stop and temperatures around 15–21°C/60–70°F are optimum.

Philodendron augustisectum is a climber with leaves that are deeply dissected up to 40cm (16in), the higher up the plant the more dissected they tend to be. The leaves make wonderful shadows and this looks best grown as a large specimen plant. It will easily reach 2m (6ft) tall given a big enough pot.

Philodendron bipennifolium, **Fiddle-leaf philodendron**, is from Brazil. It is another climber with handsome very large leaves divided into 5 lobes with the middle one the longest. The leaves are up to 75cm (30in) long. 'Variegatum' has creamy variegated leaves and 'Burgundy' has very dark red leaves.

Philodendron melanochrysum, **Velour philodendron**, is from Colombia. Its large, long, heart-shaped leaves are dark olive green and velvety looking. The leaves can grow up to 75cm (30in) long, but 20cm (8in) is more average in a pot. The veins, leaf edges and margins are picked out in a paler green and the underside of the leaf is a pinkish-purple. It is a climber and, given a pole or something to clamber, will reach 2m (6ft) tall.

Philodendron scandens, **Heart-leaf** or **Sweetheart plant** (pictured), is the most popular. It can either be grown as a climber up a moss or coir pole or grown as a trailer. The leaves are very shiny, up to 15cm (6in) long with a perfect heart shape. It is easy enough to get this one mixed up with the pothos vine, but the young leaves are a delicate bronze-green. The plant can be regularly pinched at the growing tip to encourage the plant to branch out. It can grow up to 1.5m (4ft6in) long in a pot. It prefers indirect, but bright, light conditions.

SPRING SUMMER AUTUMN WINTER

Dracaena marginata, Dragon plant, Asparagaceae

I have a bit of hard time with *Dracaena* merely because I don't like them. Or I like them wild, but in a house they make me think of neglect. They are too often those thin-leaved, slightly spiky things with a trunk covered in a bit of wax at the top with a thick layer of dust and no one has watered them for 6 months. They are incredibly tolerant of erratic, poor watering. You can get away with little or no water for months (6 months might be pushing it) and at the first drop of moisture the plant picks up again. But plants that are tortured look it; they are droopy and the leaves are lacklustre and pale as they start to mine their resources to stay alive – the thick, grey trunk may begin to sag. If you see a houseplant by a bin on the street I can almost guarantee it's a *Dracaena*.

Still, it doesn't have to be that way. These are great plants for bright north- and east-facing rooms. They don't like direct light and are happy at temperatures around 10–24°C/50–75°F. In bright, hotter rooms you will have water them more frequently, but their drought tolerance is legendary for something that's not a

succulent. They dislike waterlogged conditions and if they get soft brown leaves or a soft trunk, the plant has been overwatered. Allow the top few centimetres (1in) of soil to dry out between watering.

Brown leaf tips are either a sign of underwatering or may mean that the plant is sitting in a cold draught, something that will make it sulk. It's normal for the bottom leaves to go yellow-brown and then fall off: this is part of the growth cycle as new leaves appear on the top. However, if all the leaves do this at once, it is a sign that the plant is going into extreme measures to deal with drought.

The trunk is often cut and then waxed to prevent it from rotting. The result of cutting the trunk is that it branches out and you get a more full head of hair. You don't half see some strange bendy ones as the plants strain for light and if you find that your plant is getting a little leggy, it needs more light. They do best in indirect light, but they certainly struggle in shade. You can cut back the trunk or stems anywhere about 10–15cm (4–6in) from the base to make it sprout but you

Dracaena marginata comes from Madagascar and can grow to considerable heights. It has thin, lanceolate leaves in glossy green with a red margin. It is often grown as a multi-stem plant and likes higher humidity than many. All *Dracaena* dislike waterlogged conditions, so if you feel you need to increase humidity, sit the plant in a saucer of water with pebbles to increase the moisture around the plant. Grouping the plant with other houseplants will also improve humidity.

***Dracaena draco*, Canary Island dragon tree**, is a native to the Canary Islands , Cape Verde, western Morocco and Madeira. Here it grows into an impressive tree known for its drought tolerance. In the house it can withstand dry atmospheric conditions, but it needs much more light then other *Dracaena*, ideally growing in bright conditions as it will grow weedy and bendy in too little light. The leaves are broadly lanceolate, light green with a slightly toothed margin. The trunk eventually turns a deep grey, but can be quite pale when young.

Anthurium, *Araceae*

Anthurium are very easy going houseplants. There are two species regularly grown indoors for their shiny heart-shaped foliage and strange waxy flowers, spathes and arched or twisted spadix. Both species are native to tropical rainforests of South America and like warm, humid environments in bright, but indirect light. They must be shaded from hot summer sun and are ideal bathroom plants. They prefer porous compost with some bark added for drainage and aeration. If you can't do this, make sure you poke the soil with a chopstick so that it gets good aeration as they thrive on this. They will need regular watering and a misting once in a while throughout the growing season, fertilising every 2–4 weeks. When the light levels and temperature drop, water less, but so that the soil is just moist and never completely dries out. If you find that you are getting very small leaves it's a sign that the plant needs repotting.

may need loppers or a saw as the trunk can be quite thick. Water the plant and then don't let it get bone dry, but ease it back into growth with sparse watering. New growth will appear in 2–3 weeks.

Dracaena thrive if fed regularly. Liquid feed them every two weeks in the summer and you'll get a very healthy plant. They are sensitive to an excess of fluoride that can make the leaves turn yellow and scorched, so if you think this is happening use rainwater for a bit to flush the excess nutrients out of the soil. However, it's more likely that the plant is in too much sun or underwatered.

They are poisonous to pets and *Dracaena marginata*, with its grass-like foliage, seems particularly enticing, even to cats.

Dracaena fragrans is native throughout tropical Africa, where it grows as a multi-stemmed shrub in the understorey of montane forests (also know as moist forests). It prefers temperatures of 18–24°C/65–75°F and likes fairly high humidity, but in the house it can cope with varying conditions, but it doesn't like direct light. It has broad, glossy green, lanceolate leaves and in the wild produces highly fragrant flowers but it is very rare to see these indoors.

Draecena fragrans 'Janet Craig' (pictured on page 168) is a popular variety and rated one of the best plants to remove indoor air pollution by Nasa.
Draecena fragrans 'Lemon Lime' is a popular variegated variety with cream, yellow and lime stripes to the leaves.
Draecena fragrans 'Warneckii' has white and green variegated stripes to the leaves.

Anthurium andreanum likes warmth and humidity to do best and will produce an impressive clump with lush, shiny foliage and flowers regularly if well fed and happy. It has a brilliant bright red, waxy spathe and arched, white spadix which has tiny yellow flowers. It prefers temperatures above 13°C/55°F.

Anthurium scherzerianum, **Flamingo flower** can survive temperatures slightly lower than *A. andreanum* though it does best in humid conditions to flower well. It has glossy, lance-shaped leaves and the flower structure is a distinctive orange-red spadix spiralling from the top of the spathe which is usually red.

Index

Index

Acknowledgements

Many thanks to Charlotte Harris for letting me fill her house with plants and never once complaining that there wasn't really room for more. Thanks to Jin at Conservatory Archives for creating a houseplant shop from heaven and then letting us photograph it. To John Hoirns at Crocus.co.uk for his excellent advice, good humour and sending lots of lovely plants to photograph. And to Mark at Violet Grey for the beautiful steps.

To Simon Wheeler for his lovely photographs (which sort of goes without saying) and his kind, good humour. To Sophie Allen for being the best editor of the bunch and Damian Jaques for making the book look so beautiful. And to Christian Tate for the brilliant illustrations.

Finally to my mum, who gave me my first houseplant.